Praise for *My So-Called Digital Life*
Created by Bob Pletka

"*My So-Called Digital Life* is an ambitious project, an attempt to map from the inside the daily experience of adolescence. . . . If *My So-Called Digital Life* has a defining message, it's that our children are more like us than we know."—David L. Ulin, book editor, *Los Angeles Times Book Review*

"Adults and teens will come away stirred and enlightened by this raw, impressive student collaboration and by Pletka's moving introduction, which challenges administrators to rethink how school is taught. YA: Teens will be fascinated by these words and images from their peers."—*Booklist*

"The resulting volume is slick, busy, and energetic in its candid presentation of emblematic teen moments . . . the volume could provide an excellent model for similar projects undertaken at the local level. Adults should take their time reading and viewing this work in order to get a real inside view of what life is like for the 21st-century teen— and what the contemporary teen journalist finds to be compelling subject matter."—*Kliatt*

"A beautifully produced book of big, bold collages of photographs accompanied by short quotes and a few longer passages, written and formatted by the participants. . . . The student insights are perceptive, from the pros and cons of surveillance cameras, to the frustrations accompanying unreliable technology, to the effects of iron bars surrounding their schoolyards. Prevalent themes include boredom, lack of sleep, and worry as students tell of an educational system that has substituted copying and repetition for inspiration and creativity. The bright spots in teens' lives seem to be extracurricular activities, particularly music and sports. They write very clearly about the life lessons (not to mention joy) that they gain from both. Is this a book for adults or teens? Although Pletka addresses his introduction to adults and even the student writers seem to be appealing for change, it should find a wide teen audience. What teenager does not enjoy seeing how peers live? One hopes that they will pass it on to their parents."— *VOYA* (Voice of Youth Advocates) Magazine

"As a whole, this book serves as a broad, almost panoramic collage of the edgy, high-tech lives of teenagers in the early 21st century. An invigorating blend of humor and insight, it is recommended for all libraries where there is interest in student photography."—*Library Journal*

"An honest, colorful and poignant book. It captures high school life the way it really is, not the shiny way you see it on Fox."—*San Diego Union-Tribune*

"*My So-Called Digital Life* zooms in on teenage life in the new millennium."—*Boston Herald*

"Every picture tells a story, the saying goes. The pictures in *My So-Called Digital Life* tell about something that few parents of teens ever get to hear: What happened in school today?"—*Orange County Register*

"Reveals a world in which it is a real struggle to maintain hope."—World Wide Work (American Labor Education Center)

"The pictures range from breathtaking landscapes to kids falling asleep in class. They reflect teen issues such as body image, feeling trapped, and how to have fun. . . . The photos reveal that teens are resilient and have a sense of humor about their situations."—*San Gabriel Valley Tribune*

"An impressive photo essay that documents the daily lives of California high school students to inspire your next photo project."—*CollegeBound Teen* magazine

"Although the book is geared toward helping parents understand what life is like for teens in the 21st century, teens will find commonality amid the unfiltered views of their peers."—*San Diego Family Magazine*

EDUCATING THE NET GENERATION

HOW TO ENGAGE STUDENTS IN THE 21ST CENTURY

Bob Pletka, Ed.D.
Creator of *My So-Called Digital Life*

SANTA
MONICA
PRESS

EDUCATING THE NET GENERATION

HOW TO ENGAGE STUDENTS IN THE 21ST CENTURY

Bob Pletka, Ed.D.
Creator of *My So-Called Digital Life*

2773923

Copyright ©2007 by Bob Pletka

SANTA
MONICA
PRESS

Published by: Santa Monica Press LLC
P.O. Box 1076
Santa Monica, CA 90406-1076
1-800-784-9553
www.santamonicapress.com
books@santamonicapress.com

Printed in the United States

Santa Monica Press books are available at special quantity discounts when purchased in bulk by corporations, organizations, or groups. Please call our Special Sales department at 1-800-784-9553.

ISBN-13 978-1-59580-023-7
ISBN-10 1-59580-023-9

Library of Congress Cataloging-in-Publication Data

Pletka, Bob.
  Educating the net generation : how to engage students in the 21st century / by Bob Pletka.
— 2nd ed.
     p. cm.
  Includes bibliographical references.
  ISBN-13: 978-1-59580-023-7
  ISBN-10: 1-59580-023-9
  1. Generation Y—Education—United States. 2. High school students—Attitudes—United States. 3. High school dropouts—United States. I. Title.

LA227.4.P58 2007
373.18—dc22

                                                                2007015198

Cover and interior design and production by cooldogdesign.

Cover photo by June Marie Sobrito ©Jms/Dreamstime.com.

CONTENTS

ACKNOWLEDGMENTS

I WISH TO ACKNOWLEDGE Dr. Amy Gimino, whose support, kindness, and belief in me gave me the confidence I needed to continue.

I want to thank my dear wife, Eileen, and my children, Clare and David, who supported me throughout the writing and research of this project. I could have never done this without their love. Clare and David, you are the hope of our family.

I wish to thank Dr. Shahnaz Lotfipour and Dr. Nancy Christensen, who engaged me in the research culture of the university. You invited me to become someone more than who I was.

Finally, I want to acknowledge and thank my publisher Jeffrey Goldman, who believed in my kids and in this project. Through his belief, he changed the lives of hundreds of kids and gave them hope for a future some didn't think they had.

THE ROLE OF INFORMATION AND COMMUNICATION TECHNOLOGY IN OUR CHILDREN'S LIVES

MY DAUGHTER AND I WERE at the breakfast table having a conversation, and I asked her about school. She told me that her teacher was having them read a story from their Basal reader four times so that the class would be able to memorize all the details from the story for the test. "However," she continued, "if I tell you something, will you promise not to get mad? I have a tally sheet. I count my yawns during the class. Yesterday was a new record—43 yawns in one day." Despite the good grades she was getting, I was concerned by my daughter's disengagement and disinterest.

Her experience of disinterest is common to the Net Generation, who are disengaging and dropping out from our anachronistic schools at some of the highest rates in 40 years. In this nation, one in three students drops out of school, and almost two in three high school students are continuously disengaged from classroom learning. The recent National Governors Association Task Force cited the 32% student dropout rate as the largest problem facing education today because of its potential to hinder the future growth of the United States as an economic power. Additionally, Susan Patrick, former Director of Education Technology of the U.S. Department of Education, suggests that 80% of future jobs will require postsecondary education, and that the rising dropout rate as well as the low percentage of students persisting in college (only 28% by sophomore year) will prevent many of our students from competing for jobs. To resolve the dropout problem, extreme solutions are being proposed nationwide. For example, the mayor of Los Angeles has campaigned to strip the L.A. School District of its authority and transfer governance to the City of Los Angeles, as other mayors have done in Chicago and New York. Mayor Antonio Villaraigosa cites the 50% dropout rate in Los Angeles Unified as one of the major reasons he should take over the district.

School reform is needed because public schools arose during an agriculture era, adapted to an industrial age, but have been slow to adapt to

"In the battle for teenagers' minds and attention, the lure of your own personal soundtrack often wins out."

the needs of an information and communication society. The outspoken critic, former CEO, and educational philanthropist Bill Gates recently made derisive commentary about today's high schools saying, "Training the workforce of tomorrow with today's high schools is like trying to teach kids about today's computers on a 50-year-old mainframe." His concerns are shared by the American Youth Policy Forum, which criticized high schools by finding that "while the world around us continues to change at unprecedented rates, most high schools have been slow or resistant to change." Not only are the curriculum and content in question, but the process by which the Net Generation is educated is also suspect. Because the Net Generation has been shaped by an environment that is information and communication rich, team-based, achievement-oriented, visually based, and instantly responsive, they often recoil from isolated, lectured-based, information-dated, responsive-deficient silos of learning comprised of outdated technologies from the mid-20th century.

This issue of student disengagement and dropout has become extremely personal as I've struggled to deal with it as an educator, researcher, and father. As an administrator in a school district, I work with certain at-risk populations that have a historical dropout rate of 55%. I also work with a committed group of teachers dedicated to making a difference, and who struggle with youths that are angry, lonely, economically disadvantaged, and often substance dependent. As a researcher, I have conducted a recent study in which I interviewed hundreds of high school and middle school students about their experience at school and have been troubled to hear how the majority of them disengage from learning by spending their classroom time sleeping, talking, daydreaming, or listening to their iPod. One student wrote that "in the battle for teenagers' minds and attention, the lure of your own personal soundtrack often wins out."

As a father, I find it particularly disturbing how personal this problem has become. This year my normally curious and healthy 10-year-old son started getting a mysterious illness that had no symptoms other than a whine that emitted from his lips whenever he opened his mouth to talk. This ailment chronically struck Monday mornings before school. On a more serious note, my 13-year-old daughter recently told me she was not planning to pursue any career that involved math and then asked me how many years of math she "had" to take in high school. Being a former math teacher, I let her know that she'd be taking four years of mathematics that included algebra, geometry, and trigonometry and, if she were lucky, she would get the opportunity to take Advanced Placement Calculus. I realized that my terse response might have failed to resolve the underlying problem. After calming myself, what I found worried me even more—she let me know that even though she was getting an A, she didn't understand what she was doing. She had simply memorized the algorithms to prepare for her tests but had failed to comprehend the concepts underlying the math formulas. She felt frustrated and was trying to escape from her feeling of failure. Because she was retreating from the possibility of math in her future, she was also disengaging.

The subject of student withdrawal and disinterest is one facet of the issue of student dropout. Even though all of us—parents, educators,

"Who wants to spend hours finding answers out of the text and just copying it down? It has already been written—why write it again?"

policymakers, and community members—may face this situation in varying degrees, this is a problem that all of us share and need to resolve. We all have a stake in education because the education that our sons and daughters receive will shape our future nation.

Meaningless Schoolwork Contributing to the Problem

The problem of student disengagement is rooted in the quality of instruction and learning. Most secondary school students perceive the work they do in school as meaningless. In a recent study, students expressed that their predominant experience of school was completing worksheets, copying notes, and listening to lectures. They wondered what the point was of these futile exercises. One student described this sense of futility as follows: "Who wants to spend hours finding answers out of the text and just copying it down? It has already been written—why write it again?" Another student told me, "Unfortunately school . . . is but cramming knowledge and repetitive exercises. All for the sake of building up skill. . . . To no surprise many end up dozing off over books." As a result of this sense of futility, students disengage or, as one student wrote, "Students begin to question themselves, their abilities and their potential."

These perceptions are typical of most students: almost two-thirds of secondary school students ultimately become disconnected from learning. This coincides with the two-thirds of students who drop out from school. The students who drop out frequently cite irrelevant coursework as the reason. This increasing perception that school is of no value is a contributing factor to the rise in student disengagement and student dropout rates.

Many of us from previous generations can remember back to our own school days and may remember classmates with similar feelings. However, in the last 20 years the numbers of students who find school-work meaningless has risen another 12%. Additionally, the number of student dropouts has also risen from about 23% in 1969 to its current rate of 32%. Not surprisingly, the increasing rate of students who find no meaning in school corresponds to the rising rates of students who drop out and disengage from learning.

Belonging and Collaboration

In addition to the meaninglessness that students cited in school, the National Dropout Prevention Center and Network found that student alienation is strongly correlated to high dropout rates. If students perceive they don't belong, they are more likely to disengage and drop out. This loneliness and isolation may be surprising since the high school experience is typically rich in various social opportunities such as athletics, band, clubs, and leadership positions that could arguably create a sense of community, meaning, and interaction. However, according to researchers Liethwood, Jantzi, and Haskell, 46% of the variation in the students' sense of involvement and belonging is the result of instruction. Whereas instruction dominated by lectures and note taking is associated with increased rates of disengaged students, lessons that encourage student discussion contribute to their sense of acceptance and membership in school. Despite the many potential opportunities for community building outside of the classroom, what happens during classroom instruction does play an important, if not the most important, role in creating a sense of inclusion or, inversely, a sense of isolation.

Although research indicates collaborative learning often leads to student engagement in education, researchers Gamoran and Nystrand found that a majority of secondary classes have 15 seconds or fewer of group discussion. While 85% of all instructional activities entailed lectures or seatwork that precluded students from interacting with one another, only 1% of class time was devoted to collaborative learning. In a recent study, one student asserted: "The only interaction that happens during the course of the day is the teacher writing on the white board as you stare at the back of her head trying to hear the soft mumbles over the distractions throughout the room."

This experience is typical of most students. In the 2005 High School Survey of Student Engagement (HSSE), 52% of students expressed that they had not discussed any ideas from their readings or classes for the entire school year. The opportunities that students have to dialogue, collaborate, and build knowledge about essential questions with their peers and teachers are important to students and ultimately influence whether they actively participate in learning. The quality of the relationships that students have in class with their peers and teachers is important to their success in school.

Despite the strong research that shows socially contextualized learning engages students, researchers such as Jones, Jones, and Hargrove found that teachers are lecturing more and discussing less. Because almost every state in the nation has adopted high stakes testing in an attempt to comply with the national educational policy No Child Left Behind and to provide the public with a much needed accountability system, educators are narrowing their range of instructional methods and becoming more entrenched in teacher-centered instructional practices such as lecturing and note taking. Because high stakes accountability measures can significantly affect schools financially (in the forms of incentives or punishments), instructors often use inferior teaching methods.

Although these strategies are associated with higher rates of student disengagement, teachers perceive these strategies as more effective at preparing students to learn the basic skills assessed by high stakes testing. Teachers are able to move quickly through the large amounts of content standards in which students are tested even though students have not had opportunities to apply the content in meaningful contexts. This rise in teacher-centered practices of lecturing and note taking, as well as the decrease in student-centered methods that emphasize constructing meaning and interacting with others, may help explain the rise in student dropouts. Ironically, a generation that needs and expects a greater sense of collaboration and interaction is getting less of these than previous generations did.

The Net Generation

Because the Net Generation has been shaped by a communication- and information-rich environment, youths expect environments that enable them to collaborate with others in their own community and with a larger global network. Their need for a sense of community, teamwork, and collaboration has been combined with a world that has become digitized and computerized. The new digital frontier enables them to connect to diverse sectors, friends close or geographically distant, and

new commercial markets through computers, PDAs or cell phones. When 84% of teenagers own at least one personal digital device to call, text or instant message their friends, or to email relatives for advice, the use of technology to create these connections is important to their sense of belonging and inclusion in society.

While members of the Net Generation may have greater opportunities for connecting to community and friends through their ubiquitous access to communication technologies outside of class, their experience of isolated classroom learning starkly contrasts with their typically connected life and may exacerbate feelings of alienation and separation. Despite the 98% of schools that are physically connected to the Internet, the renowned educational technology researcher Larry Cuban found that, nationwide, only 20% of teachers use information and communication technologies as part of their instruction. Classrooms remain relatively unchanged by the information era. The differential between continuous connection outside of class and isolated alienation during class is readily apparent to the students. As this student wrote about her classroom experience, "Now I see the loneliness that has surrounded me."

Net Generation Different from Earlier Generations

The Net Generation is different from their Generation X parents and Baby Boomer grandparents. As birth rates rose in this youngest generation, doting parents and grandparents, who desperately wanted offspring, protected the Net Geners. This group of children is seen as precious by their parents and society, who responded to their kids by customizing and personalizing the world for them. From their favorite color of juice (blue, red, and orange) to the entertainment they watch (Nickelodeon, Disney, and MTV) to the customized home for their extracurricular activities (game rooms, athletic facilities, and mini dance studios), this generation has always felt special. This world sharply contrasts with the one in which their Generation X parents were raised.

The cynical Gen X'ers were born to broken, divorced, *Kramer vs. Kramer* parents who didn't have time to raise their latchkey children.

Net Generation youths are also different from their Baby Boomer grandparents. Net Generation youths are cooperative team players who multitask and connect with others through ongoing text, instant, voice, or video messaging. They are digital natives in a world of evolving information and communication technologies (ICT) made for their interaction with all sectors of society. They are comfortable with the conventions of society and even the authority of adults and parents who often direct their lives. In contrast, the Baby Boomer grandparents grew up to become independent, rule-breaking, creative thinkers. Strauss and Howe in their book *Millennials Rising* argue that the GI generation reacted to fascism and communism from the World Wars by discouraging their children, the Baby Boomers, from becoming rule-following, authority-oriented, conventional adults. They feared their children would be manipulated by charismatic, fascist leaders who might take advantage of eager followers.

Unlike previous generations, whose experiences drew pictures one at a time in a linear fashion on the mind's tabula rasa, the Net Generation's

experiences rasterized multiple images simultaneously on their mind's dendritic displays. If, as John Locke proposed, our personality, character, and values are nurtured by the environment, then the Net Generation has been nurtured by a world of digital technology, instant information, global communication, and individually customized environments that has made them different from any previous generation. Digital technology has been embedded into every area of society from relationships to commerce. This new world has nurtured most to become comfortable multitasking and to expect experiential, dynamic, and cooperative activities facilitated through information and communication technologies. With this background, we should not be surprised that when this Net Generation enters our classrooms—notorious for their cultures of isolation combined with their lack of technology—students may find these places of learning irrelevant. As one student wrote: "Even though we're entering the 21st Century, school has barely changed since the last century."

Solutions to the Problem

To address the problem of student dropout and disengagement, the National Dropout Center suggests using instructional technologies to extend classroom collaborative activity beyond the confines of the class itself to allow meaningful discussion with professionals, practitioners, and community members. This recommendation comes from research that finds authentic activities that extend beyond the classroom into communities of practice can enhance student participation and promote a sense of belonging and engagement.

Eighth graders at Brunswick Junior High School in Brunswick, Maine, are engaging in an authentic activity when they interact with scientists at NASA in order to study weather in a collaborative learning context. These students employ the same tools used by the community of NASA meteorologists to solve weather pattern problems. Students take satellite photographs of different weather systems using EarthKAM, a camera on the International Space Station, and then collaborate with the EarthKAM community to interpret and speculate about the scientific meaning and significance of these pictures. As students grapple with questions through ongoing online dialogue, their learning is supported by the expertise and guidance of those with greater knowledge and experience. Through this support and guidance, student engagement and understanding are enhanced.

The theoretical foundations upon which information and communication technology (ICT) projects are based, such as Vygotsky's 1978 cultural-historical perspective and Wenger and Lave's 1991 situated learning study, help explain why these applications are likely to enhance the effectiveness of teaching and learning in the K-12 context. Vygotsky's and Wenger and Lave's theories explain learning as an active and communal process whereby students build knowledge and construct meaning through interaction with others. Thus, both see learning as fundamentally connected to the social context. Within the school environment, parents, teachers, and children interact, helping the learner internalize knowledge. Beyond the school walls, these interactions help the learner hone his or her communication skills through interactions within the cultural context of the larger community. Lave and Wenger and Vygotsky argue that this culturally contextualized engagement within a community is critical for learning. Furthermore, because ICT applications enable students to collaborate with communities of practitioners beyond the school walls, students are likely to engage in contextualized learning that they find meaningful.

Whereas Lave, Wenger, and Vygotsky argue that the social context is critical to learning, Mark Warshauer expands upon their argument by suggesting that it is the use of ICT that helps students connect to that sociocultural context. ICTs, such as Computer Supported Collaborative Learning (CSCL), are critical to sectors of society, commerce, and government. As such, students' use of ICT is ethically imperative for their full inclusion into society. ICT helps students fully communicate and interact with others in society, and through these interactions, students become participating members of society.

As I examined the breadth of research on ICT and its relationship to student disengagement and dropout, I found myself asking more unanswered questions. I wanted to understand what students' learning

experiences are like and the extent to which a sense of belong
gagement occur. Additionally, I wanted to further understan
educational ICT could develop a sense of community, not only with
other students but also with adult practitioners such as publishers, writers,
and photographers who would serve to mentor the students. Because
inclusion and engagement imply a relationship between people, I reasoned
that collecting data about the perceptions of those involved—students and
the community members—would be important to determine whether
ICT does indeed mediate student inclusion into a community.

With this need in mind, I identified an opportunity to study a school
technology project, My So-Called Digital Life. The project was comprised
of 2,000 teenage students who engaged in learning language arts standards
using ICT to connect them to professional photographers, scholars,
publishers, and graduate students for the purpose of mentoring. This
multidimensional project guided students through the writing process
using digital photography as a catalyst for writing. Students in grades six
through twelve across the state of California participated in a five-week
endeavor in which they took photographs of their classroom learning
experiences, school, and community. Afterwards, students wrote blogs
about their photographs and, through their pictures and words, were able
to share their community and school experiences with other students.
Students then selected one photograph that they believed best repre-
sented their typical experience and wrote a narrative essay about it.

Throughout the process, community experts, including photographers, writers, and researchers, supported and assisted the students in the
simulation through email, online discussions, and electronic media
resources. Each student was paired with an expert who sent a minimum
of three emails whereby the expert engaged the student in continuing online
dialogue, provided online media resources, and critiqued the student's
work. At the end of the five-week project, the photographs, captions, and
student narratives were compiled into an edited book, which was published
by Santa Monica Press and then distributed back to all participating classes
(as well as being distributed nationally). Similar to the findings from other
researchers, the students in the project reported that they engaged in

meaningful learning where their connection and communication with other students, mentors, and professionals supported their studies.

Even though the findings from the study produced rich data that helps to explain student disengagement and dropout, I find that my role as a parent is what gives me the will to take action to address the dual problems. As a father, I want to inspire and instill a passion for learning that propels my son and daughter to be curious and to ask questions that enable them to build their understanding and knowledge about their identity, relationships, community, and environment. However, the legacy of the renowned educator John Dewey challenges me to extend my moral imperative as a father to my action as an educator for all students in my schools: "What the best and wisest parent wants for his child must be what the entire community wants for all its children." Or, as the researcher Carl Glickman said, "We need to love all our students like we love our own children." From this commitment to all children of our community, together parents, community leaders, educators, students, employers, researchers, and policymakers can transform the mediocrity of secondary education into a purposeful and meaningful endeavor. This commitment to all children is important because the schools we create today will shape the American identity of tomorrow.

CHAPTER 1

THE EMERGING NET GENERATION

LISTENING TO A VIBRANT speaker, self-identified from the Silent Generation, give a presentation on generational differences, I found that most of his talk resonated with me. This feeling shifted, however, when he began speaking about the Net Generation and their ubiquitous use of technology, arguing that because of their reliance on digital communication, they would surely find themselves feeling lonely and isolated from the real world. Even though his words had seemed somehow comforting to me as he reaffirmed my world view and suggested that we were not the ones who needed to adapt, his words no longer resonated. He went on to say that he "found it amusing that this generation would rather text message than speak to a person face to face." Rhetorically, he asked the audience, "How will they be able to procreate?" (Somehow, I doubted this would be a problem for the generation.) Another person from the audience, a Baby Boomer, commented that she found it disturbing when she saw members of the Net Generation talking on the cell phone instead of talking to the person next to them. She and the speaker both concluded, with agreement from much of the audience, that the Net Generation would rather communicate and interact using technology in the virtual world than interact face to face in the real world.

I found the audience's conclusion more insightful of our own generation's underlying perceptions of the world than about the underlying ptions of the Net Generation. The perception is that somehow the world is divided into the real and the virtual and, additionally, that face-to-face interactions within social, economical, religious, and political contexts are deemed meaningful whereas digital online communication and interaction is a playful diversion from the real world. While the audience may have conceded that operating in this digital world could be fun, interesting, and even informative, many of them stated that the virtual environment separates those who enter it from the real work and meaningful interactions that come from physical contact and face-to-face meetings.

While this notion appeals to me—a division between real communication and digital interaction—this line no longer separates the world any longer (if ever). The line has blurred with a Gaussian effect in which two separate images blend. Many of us know somebody who started an online relationship that led to marriage sometime later. Real dollars and fortunes are being made and spent in virtual, multiplayer games and on e-commerce sites. Political campaigns are being waged on the web while powerful computers and satellites are used to hunt down terrorists. From making love to waging war, the two worlds of the physical and the digital have blended to form a new image of society. Digital communication does not replace face-to-face interaction, but it does create new opportunities, remove time and geographical barriers, and enable new global connections.

Even though the Net Generation perceives the digital and the physical as intrinsically linked, the aforementioned speaker's conclusion, which suggested that the Net Generation would rather text message with a friend that talk with them face-to-face, is based not on research but on the perceptions from older generations about a new rising one. It is not that Net Geners would rather instant message than spend time interacting with a friend face-to-face but rather that they have limitless possibilities with whom they can choose to communicate. For this generation, the world is all about choices—when, how, why, and what they want to communicate—and neither time nor place can stop them. When they are choosing to interact with someone over a cell phone rather than to speak with the person next to them, some Net Geners may have decided that they would rather communicate with somebody else at that moment or that the conversation has become stagnant or that the person next to

them doesn't have an answer to a question they want resolved right now. It is all about choices; but it is also about instant responses to those choices, and sometimes instantly does not come fast enough. Unfettered by constraints such as distance and time that have bound previous generations, Net Geners decide when and with whom they want to communicate moment by moment.

This perpetual ability to make choices was recently made clear on a family vacation with my wife and two children. Driving along the awe-inspiring Redwood Highway in Northern California, my wife and I were pointing out the ancient trees to our kids only to have my teenager comment that one tree seemed to look like all the rest. As we continued to admire the scenery, I noticed that my daughter had become silent and was looking down at something in her hands. It wasn't long before I realized that she was text messaging. At that moment I had to confront the brutal fact that this act did not mean she would rather communicate digitally than interact face-to-face, but that she would rather socialize with a friend about a topic of her choosing than participate in a more generalized family discussion. Ouch! She had simply chosen to take part in a communication that was more exciting than the family tree conversation her parents were having. Like no other group in history, this generation has more choices, access, and ability to choose what selections they perceive will meet their needs, tastes, and interests.

Who is the Net Generation?

So who is this emerging generation? Some call them the Millennial Generation, Generation Y, Echo Boomers, iGeneration, or the Net Generation. Born between 1982 and 2002, this group was the first to grow up in the digital and Internet era. Don Tapscott first coined the term "Net Generation" in his book *Growing Up Digital* to describe a generation shaped by a new, networked, visually rich, digitally constructed communication and information world. In this environment, all the world's locations, maps, and places can be stored digitally as 1s and 0s on a GPS small enough to be held in a child's hand. This generation was born and nurtured in an environment in which information is a commodity and a 13-year-old has the same access to the information and distribution network on the World Wide Web that the multinational billion-dollar corporation has.

As a result of growing up in this digitally constructed information and communication atmosphere, the Net Generation is most comfortable multitasking in fast-paced, visually oriented environments. In applied learning situations, they are adept at discovering information where it can be accessed randomly in associative contexts rather than in step-by-step linear ways. Whether operating within the 3-D virtual worlds of

The Net Generation spends more time playing video games and surfing the Net than watching television.

online video games or maneuvering through hyperlinked e-commerce sites such as Ebay, this generation mostly functions in these experiential online worlds competently without the need for manuals or *For Dummies* books. When they do need assistance, they expect short video clips, graphics, or collaborative contexts in which they can simply ask quick questions and get short answers to guide them through online quagmires.

Even though Net Geners expect collaborative learning conditions and social online contexts, they also expect individualized feedback to their unique needs. From changing an automated voice from male to female or switching their splash screen on their blog, they seek opportunities to personalize the world to their preferences. Many of them not only have the opportunity but also possess the technical skill and competency to customize these environments. Moreover, they have been shaped by the merging of information and communication and have become the "Digital Natives" of this new world.

Tabula Rasa—Nurtured by their Environment

Even as I write this, in my own mind I can hear my grandfather saying, "Kids are kids. What was good for previous generations will be good for future generations. If it was good enough for me then it is good enough for them." When referring to love, character, dedication, and the value of commitment, I would agree with him. However, different from previous generations are many of this generation's values (although rooted strongly in the American tradition, e.g., diversity), needs (e.g., visual learners), expectations (e.g., self-paced, customized), and skills (e.g., information literacy, digital competencies). Net Geners have been nurtured by the development of this new digital world to make them who they are.

As suggested by the empiricist philosophers Locke, Bacon, and Hume, as well as by modern psychologists such as John Watson, a person, a community of people, or, in our case, a generation of people acquire knowledge and behaviors through the experiences of the senses and as a reflection of those experiences. Their behaviors are the result of interaction and conditioning from the environment that ultimately shapes who they become. The renowned educational researchers, Lave and Wenger go further and suggest that individuals, community, and the environment are reconstituted and changed in a dialectical process of engagement by the individual within a community and the environment. The world that shaped this generation is significantly different from any previous.

So what are the new forces that have nurtured this new generation? Digital technologies have changed how information, communication, and commerce are diffused into society; but they have also nurtured a new generation of learners that have adapted to the new demands, tools, values, and expectations of an information society. In the following section, we will examine the new information, communication, and commerce environments that have shaped the generation. The section will conclude with a discussion of how the forces of information, communication and commerce digital technologies have influenced the characteristics and expectations of the Net Generation.

Information

The information rich environment that has formed the personalities and character of this generation is abundant, immediate, interactive, and always available. It is also now presented using a variety of visual, graphical, and auditory styles that provide a multitude of ways for sharing knowledge. As people interact and input information, digital systems provide instantaneous feedback and responses. Take, for example, how Nike and Apple have joined together to create a new type of multimedia workout system for the avid fitness enthusiast. With a pair of Nike Plus running shoes, a small transmitter that fits into the bottom of the shoe, and an iPod nano, a runner gets real-time feedback about his or her speed, calories burned, and distance run. Runners can have key benchmark results spoken to them through the iPod speakers while running, or they can choose to listen to a weekly podcast produced specially for these enthusiasts. When runners are wracked with fatigue and in danger of quitting, the power song starts playing through the iPod to carry them through the moment of weakness. After the workout, runners can sync the workout to the NikePlus.com website to monitor long-term progress and set goals. On the website, the enthusiast can see the workout history pop up in a graph, with an animation of a runner indicating progress. In this new online environment, personal results can be compared with others, whereby runners can compete remotely with other runners or team up with friends to set group goals. Remote results from runners are uploaded to the website, aggregating on the fly while also informing members how their team is doing.

Because the new digital world is full of systems like Nike Plus, the Net Generation has come to expect multimedia, experiential, and inter-active learning systems. They seek learning systems that provide instant feedback, such as those built into Nike Plus, so that they can adapt, acquire new skills, and collaborate with others. In their search, Net Geners have found a digital world pulsing photographs, videos, charts, text, and audio commentary that has been customized for them through speakers, displays, PDAs, multiplayer games, cell phones, headphones, and even shoes as they filter, absorb, synthesize, and distribute information yet again. They have learned to be both efficient consumers and producers of information as they create and author new knowledge and artifacts.

With the advent of online technologies such as Wiki (websites where everyone can edit content), all have the right to add to the collective knowledge of the online community. The production of books is no longer controlled solely by publishing houses; collectively, communities can now choose to author material in various genres and then distribute and market that material through the free online tools and sites of the World Wide Web. In these Wiki environments, anyone can visit the site and, with a click of the button, turn the displayed text into editable fields in which the person can change, add, or enhance what has been written. One of the most popular online encyclopedias, Wikipedia, has been completely edited, written, and produced by the public. At this moment, you could visit the Wikipedia website and add an entry about a subject in which you possess expertise, from home beer brewing to butterflies. This democratic type of access makes all of us not only consumers of knowledge but also potential producers who can contribute to the collective whole. In this setting, the youths have as much opportunity, technical skill, and access to contribute to these online works as adults with doctorates. The digital world in which they live is less about credentials and more about the content and quality of what is produced. Online environments and Wiki technologies promote the contribution of ideas, manifesting through collaborative efforts that enable outcomes and real products that are judged on their own merits within the community.

As you can imagine, this questions our assumptions about how knowledge is transferred and who has the expertise and right to contribute knowledge. What if somebody from the public adds an entry to the encyclopedia that is wrong? How do we know that it is right? Can we believe what is written (or should we)? With this technology we have found that there is a self-correcting component. Even when somebody adds a wrong entry, the community self-corrects the information as somebody adds a new entry that refutes the claim. This process does take time, from days to months, and some may question if this type of response is fast enough for an on-demand world. Expertise is no longer being defined exclusively by a Ph.D., M.D., or Ed.D. but rather by the perceived value and the quality of the idea, knowledge, or information itself. The masses are encouraged not only to consume information but also to produce new knowledge. This empowering of the individual through open access to data, production tools, and distribution networks democratizes the production of knowledge.

No longer do large oligarchies of media, publishers, governments, or local agencies have complete control over the building and allocation of information. Individuals are now empowered to compete, argue, and spread knowledge in what Thomas L. Friedman calls "the flat world." For example, the website YouTube potentially gives anyone who knows how to upload video on the Internet tremendous influence. YouTube, a website purchased by Google in which anyone can upload, download, or watch amateur or professional videos, is essentially a free distribution center for a worldwide audience. The Press Enterprise, in a November 2006 article entitled "Beating Video Shows Power of YouTube," highlighted how an alleged beating of a suspect by the police that was captured on video using a cell phone and subsequently uploaded to the YouTube website sparked an FBI investigation of the incident. After just one month of being posted on the site, 155,000 people watched the clip that helped to propel the investigation forward. Without this type of exposure, the investigation likely would not have occurred.

The power of individuals has grown as the technologies have created a synergistic effect with low-cost video cameras, inexpensive editing software, and (now) free media distribution centers on the Internet with worldwide penetration. In the past, program managers and news stations controlled the stories, opinions, video, and photographs seen and heard by the public. On an even larger scale, influential politicians, wealthy profiteers, and large media conglomerates controlled the flow of information through high-powered public relation firms and media outlets. Even as that continues today, individuals now have channels of communication that can provide them a voice to be heard by thousands of people. Many Net Geners have been given a voice in this new world, and because they have the time and access, they take advantage of technologies such as YouTube to give voice to their ideas and thoughts.

Communication

These new channels of communication have been made possible by new communication technologies, such as fiber optics, that have connected the continents of the world. Even the "last mile connection" problem is slowly being eroded as fiber optics are coming into businesses, schools, and even homes. In my community in Murrieta, California, we have fiber optics in our home that enable me to watch live events over streaming media on the Internet and participate in no cost video conferencing with our good friends in South Dakota. This trend of extending fiber optics into the home is growing throughout the country as more homes have greater bandwidth options, which bring increased media services to consumers. With fiber optics comes speed and opportunity—opportunity to interact and communicate with individuals or groups using any medium, whether it is by voice, music, multiplayer gaming, or even video conferencing.

Whereas fiber optics brought remote connectivity between continents, speed of transmission, and high quality media capacity, the increasing capability of the cell phone brings flexibility, continuous ongoing connection, and portability of information and media. For example, with the Treo, a cell phone and PDA combination, I have new ad hoc opportunities to get information and communication. During meeting presentations, I use my Bluetooth device to instant message colleagues and solicit their comments without interrupting the presenter. During breaks in the meeting, I check my email on my Treo or make a quick call. Other times, stuck waiting in a doctor's office, I'll listen to a podcast or check a website for information, all using my steroid-infused Treo cell phone. Using the built-in video camera on my phone, I have even used the device to scare off an inflamed driver who was seeking, spurred on by road rage, to use his car to ram me off the road. Since his car was inches from me, he was able to see the Treo in my hand capturing his behavior on video.

The cell phone is tremendously flexible and provides a wide range of portable media and communication services that embeds it into all aspects of society. In the past, culture was segmented by clearly defined times and tasks between the worlds of business, family, entertainment, and education. Now the cell phone acts as a hub connecting segments of people's lives. People no longer work solely from 9:00 A.M. to 5:00 P.M. at their desk or solely play on their vacation. Wherever and whenever individuals are awake, they are linked to all parts and people of their life. Our children have been shaped by this environment in which staying connected is an important value to many of them.

Most youths have this type of access and portability. For example, 70% of tweens and teenagers now have a cell phone. Whether they are checking the scores of a baseball game, ordering movie tickets, or text messaging, the cell phone is a constant part of their life. Even at school, where some administrators have banned cell phones, phones are tucked away in purses and pockets, ready to use at a moment's notice. I have heard administrators vehemently contest this fact and argue that, at their school, cell phones simply are not present, only to walk through those same sites and see evidence to the contrary. One youth wrote to me that "one of my friends asked for my cell phone number. As soon as that person said that, my other friends around me took out their cells to do the same." The cell phone has become almost another appendage and is used as naturally as their hands, without even thinking. As much as I work with digital technology, cell phones, computers, and websites, I find myself struggling to integrate ICT into my life, in contrast to the Net Generation, which lives and operates with ICT as habitually and automatically as I flip the light switch at my house. This generation has integrated ICT into their lives; it has shaped how they behave, socialize, work, think, and develop.

Commerce

The Net Generation was born primarily to Baby Boomers, who were born between 1946 and 1964, and the more cynical Generation X, born between 1964 and 1978. This youngest generation, at 80 million members, is even larger than the 77 million Baby Boomer Generation and significantly larger than the 43 million Generation X. With the size of this group, along with their large spending power of more than $485 billion annually, manufacturers and retailers have courted them. Most secondary school and college students have credit cards and are not afraid to use them. With 20% of credit card-holding students from this generation having balances over $10,000, many Net Geners are spending at voracious rates. Additionally, 40% of all Net Geners made purchases online last year with their large discretionary income. With this type of spending power, they are active and important members of the economy. In no other past generation has the youth had such discretionary income in which to influence the development of products and services in the economy. With this income, even more choices appear, as manufacturers, retailers, and advertisers tailor products and services to the tastes, interests, flavors, and values of the generation.

Because this group has both the societal freedom to make choices and the financial power to support those decisions, companies cater to this generation. Industries such as travel now have special packages for our Net Generation children. Marketing personnel from resorts know that teenagers often get to choose where the family goes on vacation, so they have services to entice children and teens. Sixty percent of families report that their children help to decide where the family will travel on vacation. Because the Net Geners often get to choose the family vacation destination, hotels like the Biltmore Resort and Spa have now personalized services just for kids, such as their new spa menu just for teenagers with "facial treatments for their oily skin." As a parent, I cannot help but think that a good bar of soap could be just as effective on their oily skin and a whole lot cheaper. However, I can hear my daughter saying that "Dad just doesn't get it."

When companies don't tailor their products to the interests of the generation, there is financial fallout. Recently, Microsoft released its version of the iPod called the Zune. The device is a portable video, graphic, and music player that has received positive reviews for its hardware specifications, with features such as its wireless music sharing capabilities. However, Fox News reports that "Microsoft's Zune Off to Slow Start at Retailers." What has been identified by Net Gener bloggers as problematic is Zune's DRV music technology that converts all of the songs stored on the device to DRV format and subsequently restricts the access to a shared song to three times in three days. This three times in three days listening capability is one way Microsoft is attempting to deal with the problem of piracy and copyright infringement; but this restriction on the Net Geners does not appear to be helping Zune sales. One blogger erroneously compared sharing music with a friend using Zune and its DRV technology to infecting the friend with a virus. (A blog is a medium of communication, a web log, that combines the personal diary with a town crier, in which 16,457 of your closest friends can read, link, and comment online. The blog becomes a powerful way to place public pressure and influence others.)

When Net Geners do not get what they want, they make other choices, communicate their preferences online, and financially impact the companies in the marketplace. Because of this impact, most corporations ultimately respond to their needs, interests, and tastes. Our Net Geners have come to expect a world that enables them to self-determine and select from an array of colors, tastes, sizes, and shapes. Unlike past generations, when children simply received what parents thought was best for them, Net Gener youths now get to decide what products and services they want. If they decide they do not want to have a portable media player that limits their choices to three times in three days, they have the cultural and financial freedom to make other choices. They simply buy what they want and then let 10,000 other people know why they selected what they did. This generation, for right or wrong, has a greater opportunity to choose than any previous group in history.

The Net Generation has tremendous choices as the world has responded to the billions of dollars that this group wields in new types of virtual, personalized settings. Largely, these digital natives have access and the ability to operate digital environments that converge the real world with the expanding online, networked environs that empower this generation to shape and bend the marketplace, community, and culture with their financial, aesthetic, and productive power. They are an emerging and rising power in society.

Experiential and Exploratory

What types of choices do our youths make, and what criteria do they use to guide their choices? When Net Geners do make choices, they usually select experiential and exploratory activities because this generation likes to learn by doing and interacting. Sitting still reflecting on an activity is an anathema to them. This generational reality became clear on a Saturday morning as our family was getting ready to go to my son's soccer game. Right before we were to leave, when my son asked me how long the trip would be to the game, I told him that it would be about 30 minutes. He responded by asking me if he could bring the portable DVD player since his Nintendo DS wasn't charged. We were rushing out, so I told him that he could not bring it, but he could grab his iPod for the trip. He gave me his most forlorn look and said, "I'll have nothing to do." As a member of another generation, I wondered what happened to the activity of looking out the window while driving through new geographies and communities. I just did not understand how 30 minutes of inactivity was a problem.

From playing on their Nintendo DS, to mixing their own hip hop files, to creating their own blogs, to arranging a virtual wedding, members of the Net Generation thrive on digital information and communication activity. Their first choice is interacting online and then, only as a last resort, watching a DVD movie. This group spends more time online than watching television. They are not satisfied sitting idly while watching mass media. They spend their three hours (on average) of online time interacting, participating in multiplayer games, communicating on social networks, building MySpace pages, and creating playlists for their iPods. When they are watching television, they prefer shows like *American Idol*, which allow them to interact and use messaging technologies that help determine the outcome. Additionally, the Net Generation does not simply watch television but explores character backgrounds and future story plots, downloads podcasts, and messages online with other viewers on blogs from authorized and unauthorized television websites.

Unlike Generation X, which first started watching MTV music videos, Net Geners experience so much more and watch so much less. To appeal to this group's need for interactive, participatory media, stations like MTV converge traditional mass media with more interactive forms of digital technology. Viewers can become part of video-game tournaments, instant message with other viewers, upload their own music videos, or download ringtones for their cell phone from Beyonce or Justin Timberlake. As an example of this media strategy, MTV holds 3-D multiplayer video game competitions on their website; the top players are selected to participate in a live-aired television tournament. Additionally, viewers have an opportunity to create their own mockumentary, animation, or comedy, with the top production airing on their station's shows, like the *G-Hole*.

For the younger Net Geners, stations like Nickelodeon invite children to visit their website and create their own animation scene with interactive creatures and props from the television station's cartoons, such as *Avatar*. This generation doesn't want to simply watch others, they want to participate. Whether it is MTV, which encourages viewers to upload

their own home-created videos, or network news asking for viewers to upload raw video footage or photographs, traditional mass media is adapting to the style of this new generation.

Multitasking

Members of the Net Generation, such as my son, accelerate their opportunities for entertainment, learning, and working by multitasking with several types of media, projects, and tasks at one time. This generation will be instant messaging while listening to their iPod and surfing the web. The research does show that the Net Generation will almost always be doing some other online activity while they are instant messaging. In Dr. Brown's study, he found that Net Geners were able to quickly change between tasks. This ability to multitask with media transfers into productivity in the workplace. In findings from another study, the Steelcase Workplace Survey, the Net Generation was found to be more adept at multitasking on the job than other generations. The findings suggest they were less likely to be distracted by noise, more capable of working in a variety of contexts, and more likely to work while traveling than other generational workers. After reading this study, I could not help but think of my own aforementioned attitude about my son's impatience and his need to multitask during the lonnnggg 30-minute drive to his soccer game. One day my perception about his impatience may be reframed by the Net Generation's future employers, who see it as a strength because those like him are able to accelerate learning and productivity by multitasking in a variety of contexts and places.

Digitally Collaborative

The other day my daughter was supposed to have two of her girl-friends over to our home, but at the last minute, one of the girls cancelled. After some time at the house, my daughter and her friend each logged on to one of the family computers and began instant messaging as they sat side by side with the laptops resting on their crossed legs. Among the tapping of keys, giggling, and commenting, the two were instant messaging each other and their absent friend. This seemed so foreign to me, a digital immigrant to their era; I could not imagine inviting friends over only to get on the computer and use it to connect socially with other friends. Being curious, I asked them why they were instant messaging. My daughter's friend responded by telling me they wanted to find out what happened to the other girl so they decided to connect up with her online. Whereas many of us from other generations may have been able to do this technological feat of instant messaging, most of us would not have wanted to interrupt a social event with what would seem to be impolite conduct toward present guests. However, to the two girls, this was as socially acceptable as playing a card game, taking a walk together, or turning on the television to watch *Monday Night Football* together.

This online, social world has evolved from people communicating online with simple text messages to interacting with virtual Avatars (3-D animated characters) through which people speak, text message, and even build new worlds. Recently, my daughter introduced me to a whole new social world of interacting Avatars in which real people use their virtual Avatar to meet others. The world is so compelling that people are paying real money for virtual property, including vehicles, in order to create online space for their interacting characters at web portals such as http://www.secondlife.com. Adults and teens have the opportunity to create virtual personas through which they are able to enter an online world. Some public speakers use their Avatar to give speeches, designers to share and sell graphics, drivers to race cars, and professors to give lectures to their students in this world.

This new social world of ICT brings up new challenges for parents and educators. One evening, I looked over my daughter's shoulder as she worked on the computer, and I noticed that she was enhancing her Avatar with blond hair and delicate features similar to her own. However, I was slightly embarrassed to see that my 13-year-old was endowing her character with certain features that were substantially larger and out of proportion to the rest of her virtual body. I wasn't quite sure how to react and simply said, "Oh!" and walked away. I was concerned about this for the rest of the evening and into the next day. I wrestled with the moral implications of this and my fatherly duty. Even though her character was only virtual, what message would she be communicating to others with her simulated plastic surgery (and new, well-endowed features) in this online world? This sentiment was counterbalanced with thoughts about what could be the harm of a developing girl exploring the concept of her own growth and maturation in a virtual world. It was not real after all.

After 24 hours of thinking about this, the next evening, sure of what I would say, I walked over to her while she was on the computer only to find her Avatar appropriately proportioned. I was relieved that she had made this decision but also uncomfortable by my own indecision and the length of time it took me to explore my own moral compass on this issue. I wondered how I would be able to guide my own daughter in this new digital world in which, at times, I do not even yet know what the moral questions are, let alone what the right answers might be. Whereas I would not have struggled with this moral decision in the real world, I was struggling with it in the virtual world. Later in the evening (wanting to be subtle), I asked her what criteria she used in building her Avatar. She answered that "the characters that people build in Second Life communicated who the person behind the Avatar was." She had wanted her Avatar to accurately communicate who she was and what she valued (she may have also decided to alter her character to meet her father's standards). Whereas I had a difficult time deciding what the right moral decision might be because I perceived the real world and virtual world as separate, she made the decision easily because for her, the virtual world was an extension of the physical world. Thus, what truly continues to separate the generations is not technological skill but how the generations perceive the digital world. Members of the Net Generation are not merely digital explorers and pioneers as many from our passing generation have become but they are natives in this land in which they were born and to which we immigrated.

CHAPTER 2

OBSOLESCENCE AND MEDIOCRE SCHOOLS

AS AN EDUCATOR, I HAVE HEARD many public indictments over the years about the failure of public schools. Even though there are cases in which schools or even school districts have failed to help students to learn, my own past experience refutes the notion of utter failure (some may say I'm splitting hairs) since I have seen many schools doing an adequate job of teaching students to read and perform rudimentary arithmetic, as well as helping them to achieve basic scores on standardized exams. Usually when I hear the hyperbole, I dismiss the comments as sound bites by those looking for an easy score with the public. However, I recently read Thomas L. Friedman's book *The World Is Flat*, a brief history of the 21st century that provided some real insight into how the curriculum needs to change and how it fails to meet the new demands of economic globalization. One quote from his book was particularly damning: "Of course, average [students] . . . are still plentiful, no doubt about it. Most of them were made that way. They were shaped in large measure by school systems that have had, from the dawn of the industrial age, a main purpose: to produce employees for boxed positions in corporate org charts that take the shape of the pyramids wide at the bottom and narrow at the top."

This searing quote rang true. He was suggesting that the school system was becoming obsolete in the new information age and that, at the very best, we were systematically producing students of mediocre ability. I would argue that there are many exceptions to this; however, largely I would have to agree with this condemnation.

Our schools do cover a large breadth of material while only expecting a demonstration of cursory understanding before moving quickly to the next standard without ever reteaching knowledge and concepts students do not master. Even our own national vision for education seems to support this idea of teaching the basics, testing the basics, and subsequently achieving only basic proficiency. Illustrating this notion, George Bush, in a recent quote, said, "The building blocks of knowledge were the same yesterday and will be the same tomorrow. . . . The basics work." This premise is hard to refute, especially for our early elementary grades. The basics of decoding sentences, comprehending text, and memorizing basic math facts are necessary and fundamental to being an educated citizen. As parents, who among us would not expect or even demand schools to teach these very essential skills?

In fact, in the late '90s, parents did begin making demands on school administrators, teachers, and politicians as parents saw many of their own children unable to read after going through the whole language program in schools. Along with these demands, the Report of the National Reading Panel: Teaching Children to Read in 2000 propelled federal, state, and local agencies into action that largely returned the teaching and learning of reading in our public schools back to a phonics-based approach. This new-old strategy has worked at our early elementary grades and has resulted in higher national reading test scores, as President Bush predicted when he said, "Teach a child to read, they'll pass the test." While this strategy has worked well to provide elementary grade levels a basic foundation, it does little to create a world-class education for our middle schools, high schools, and, arguably, even our elementary schools because the basics are, well, just that: basic, maybe mediocre, or even a little below average. We cannot confuse basics with excellence.

To further support the indictment that schools produce the average, the results from a study I conducted of secondary school students suggest something similar. In student interviews with middle and high school students, I found many expending nominal effort to cursorily complete assignments. Even though most students were willing to do the work, it was not necessarily to the best of their ability or even with a high level of effort. One student wrote: "I have noticed that many students do not do their work to the best of their ability. They will do their work, but they won't do it the best they can." Another typical student comment was: "Apathy. It's a word not quite foreign in regards to a student's attitude towards learning. It's not about succeeding, and it's not about the desire to learn. It's a desire to find the way to get through it all as easily as is humanly possible, and to figure out the easiest ways there are to attain an easy life."

One student characterized this marginal effort by writing: "Getting a C is good enough. [Parents] don't understand that Cs are plenty substantial." A second student commented, "Another thing that students do is that they cheat, students do this because they find it much easier and you don't think as much." Throughout the study I found no evidence that any student was giving his or her best effort at any time to learn the core subjects of English, math, science, and history. These findings support the results from a survey reported by the authors and researchers Strauss and Howe in their book *Millennials Rising*, which found that 65% of students don't try hard in school. Based on the findings from the study and survey, the argument should not be framed in terms of whether we teach the basics but whether knowing the basics alone helps our youth aspire to excellence (especially for those who have already achieved the basics) and, whether the basics sufficiently prepare our students to succeed in the 21st century. Thomas L. Friedman's indictment that the school system appears to produce mediocre students is not unfounded.

If we do want more from our schools and if we want to create a world-class education that prepares students to be fine citizens and economic leaders, schools need to engage students in a richer curriculum, one preparatory for jobs of the 21st century, and schools need to tailor teaching and learning strategies to the needs of the Net Generation in order to prepare them to enter the global economy of the modern age. While some may still argue that colleges and universities should be the ones to prepare students to synthesize knowledge and acquire 21st-century skills and suggest that "it is the job of K-12 schools to teach the basics of reading and writing and arithmetic," this argument would mean that only the 28% of students who make it beyond their sophomore year in college would be prepared for the work force. This leaves a large number of students without marketable skills except in local, low-paying service jobs.

Preparation for Jobs of the 21st Century

Globalization of the work force and economy has changed the requirements for what is needed from our K-12 educational institutions. In the past, the historically average students with basic skills could get jobs in Middle America and expect to earn a middle-class income. However, due to digital technologies, off shoring, outsourcing, and automation, many of the old middle-class jobs are not and will not be available. Not only is blue-collar factory work being outsourced, but many middle-class, white-collar jobs—such as those in accounting, loan management, programming, and advertising—are being outsourced to other countries that provide the labor cheaper. In order to compete, people need new skills, competencies, and talents to succeed in the global marketplace. Those workers who can create new concepts from information; add value to vanilla services; contextualize digital technologies into local markets; and connect companies, markets, and services together will be marketable in the new global work force. In *The World Is Flat*, Pulitzer Prize-winner Thomas L. Friedman lists the following needs in this new global economy:

1. Collaborators—Those who can collaborate with people between companies and among companies to facilitate global supply chains.
2. Synthesizers—Those who can put together disparate technologies to create new services and products.
3. Explainers—Those who can explain complexity into simple concepts that all can understand.

4. Leveragers—Those who can combine the best of what computers can do with the best of what people can do and reintegrate innovations.
5. Adapters—Those versatile people who can apply depth of skill to a widening scope of situations.
6. Personalizers—Those who can personalize digital services within natural human contexts.
7. Localizers—Those who can tailor global capabilities to local markets.

All of these jobs require people to apply, analyze, synthesize, evaluate, problem solve, and create new knowledge to survive. In order to succeed in these jobs, students will need 21st-century skills. The widely respected educational research organization North Central Regional Education Laboratory in 2002 reported the following 21st-century skills needed to succeed:

1. Basic Literacy—Proficiency in English and numeracy.
2. Scientific Literacy—Knowledge, comprehension, and application of scientific concepts and processes.
3. Economic Literacy—Ability to identify and analyze economic problems, incentives, and policies, as well as collect, organize and synthesize evidence.
4. Technological Literacy—Knowledge of technology, application of how it works, and purpose it serves.
5. Visual Literacy—Ability to interpret, use, appreciate, and create images and video using conventional 21st-century media in order to learn, make decisions, and communicate.
6. Information Literacy—Ability to evaluate information from a variety of media sources and synthesize information effectively using digital information and communication networks.
7. Multicultural Literacy—Ability to understand and appreciate similarities and differences in the customs, values, and beliefs of various cultures.
8. Global Awareness—Ability to recognize relationships among international organizations, sociocultural groups, and nations.

Schools need to incorporate these 21st-century skills in order to prepare students for the global work force. Simply being a reservoir of knowledge with basic competencies will not be sufficient to succeed. Workers who merely dispense information, process algorithms, and translate language will be replaced by computers or robotics or outsourced to cheaper labor in other countries. What the global economy needs are people who can create, connect, package, and explain concepts within the context of both local and global markets. Our workers will need to be continuously learning, applying, and synthesizing so that they can be part of the leading edge of innovation. For now, more than any time in our history, our youths need to become independent lifelong learners.

From Mediocrity to Obsolescence

Even though our public secondary schools sit ready to teach students, as they have for more than a century, what they are prepared to do does not meet all the new demands of the 21st century. At a governor's council, Bill Gates argued that "America's high schools are obsolete"; and while I detect some unintended hyperbole, the point is becoming more accurate with each passing day. Schools have not been retooled to meet the information, communication, or technological needs required of the information age.

Our own high school students seem to be recognizing the shift in the world, for 66% of students consider school meaningless and the same number disengage from learning. One student captured this typical perception by commenting: "Countless examples could be brought up of that enthusiastic spark disintegrating. And truly there is often no point in learning materials presented in books and worksheets. Many conclude lessons as fronts, illusions of achievements. Facts are to be learned as facts, applications aren't usually required. Necessary experience isn't gained, proving the results fruitless."

The problems of the rising dropout rate, increasing student disengagement, and decreasing relevance of the curriculum, along with the increasing need by the business community to raise the quality of education, converge to provide compelling reasons to change the structure and systems within our public schools.

Information in Our Schools

Even as there is a tremendous urgency to change the curriculum, teaching strategies, and methods of learning, we in education often maintain the current educational system without making the changes or even recognizing that adjustments are needed. If you were to go into a middle or high school, what you would see would be very similar to what you experienced in school. As one student wrote: "Schools have changed little in the last century"—from the mouth of babes.

This focus on the cycling of information from textbook and teacher to students has been reinforced by a misperception of the standards movement. I was meeting with a group of teachers who had volunteered to meet to discuss ways we could improve teaching and learning. I had mentioned to them that it was important to teach a hierarchy of thinking skills from the lower level knowledge and comprehension skills to higher level thinking skills, such as synthesis and evaluation. One woman looked at me and said, "We don't do that; we teach the state standards." This surprised me because our state has incorporated many 21st-century skills into the curriculum, as many other states have done. However, I empathize with this educator because teachers often feel obligated to teach more basic competencies due to pressure from current high stakes testing.

In the book *The Unintended Consequences of High-Stakes Testing*, written by Gail Jones, Brett Jones, and Tracy Hargrove, the authors reported most high stakes testing uses a multiple-choice format that assesses mostly lower level thinking skills such as basic knowledge and comprehension. At a more intuitive level, teachers recognize this because answers on state testing can be reduced to selecting the correct answer by bubbling in from one of four choices. This format hardly requires students to synthesize what they learn, innovate, create, or evaluate. If educators are rewarded for teaching basic competencies and either ignored or punished for teaching other higher level thinking tasks not often found on multiple-choice standardized exams, then most educators will teach what is tested. Even though the federal government has begun to recognize the importance of these skills, this recognition from the United States Secretary of Education, Margaret Spelling, is not enough even though she says "she is working to ensure that every young American has the knowledge and skills to succeed in the 21st Century" Without changing our curriculum as well as our standardized testing system to measure 21st-century skills, educators will continue to teach those abilities that are rewarded and ignore those that aren't. If we assess what we truly want our children to know, then, as President Bush says, "There's nothing wrong with teaching to the test." However, if we only test a small subset of what we want our youth to know, then teaching to the test will create an obsolete and woefully inadequate education for our children.

Student responses from the study I conducted further support the notion that secondary education has maintained the traditional means of learning without incorporating more appropriate strategies for the needs of the Net Generation. Many students perceived that lecture and note taking were the most common forms of learning in their schools. This perception is supported by other research that shows that 85% of all secondary instruction is didactic in nature (e.g., lecture and note taking). Unwittingly confirming this research, one student wrote: "My teacher is in front of the class and he is writing on the white board instructions for the period. This is the way a lot of my teachers teach. They write notes or homework on the board and it is our responsibility to write it all down."

Reading textbooks and finding answers in them were the second most predominate experiences students described. Characteristic of what many students conveyed, one student asserted, "In my learning experience we do a lot of reading out of text books that are provided . . . that is the main way we learn things in our classrooms." Added another student: "Textbooks are also a very big part of school, we are always reading out of textbooks."

In addition to reading from textbooks, students related that much of their time was spent answering questions that required them to search for answers in the textbook.

One student described a typical classroom situation using a photo he took: "In this picture the young boy reads back to the chapter where he reviews the key terms of the chapter. The teacher asked him to find the word 'feudalism' and so he opened up his book."

Another representative comment regarding textbooks was: "Scanning the book for answers, I can look through and spot answers very quick." Thus, connecting the activity of reading textbooks with the act of finding answers, students understood that it was important to retain the information that they read.. One student communicated, "As seniors we mostly write and read more because they want us to retain more information from the class." Students predominately expressed that questions they answered merely required fact-based responses found in a textbook rather than higher level reasoning that would require them to synthesize what they had learned. Not one student wrote about building knowledge, integrating, analyzing, or evaluating information. These findings are supported by other studies, such as the one by Gamoran, Nystrand and Schmoker who found that the teaching of lower level thinking skills, such as knowledge and comprehension, were the dominant skills (and in many cases the only skills) taught through the didactic strategies such as note taking, lecturing, and answering chapter questions. While these are important skills and strategies, especially for college, they are not sufficient to prepare students for the 21st century. More time is needed for writing, solving problems, and thinking critically. Ironically, whereas youths are both consumers and producers of knowledge in their lives outside of school, they are primarily consumers of knowledge (information that most students perceive as meaningless) at school. Additional strategies are needed in the classroom to demonstrate the relevance and application of their learning.

In addition to a curriculum that is insufficient to prepare students for the 21st century, the teaching methods and strategies in schools do not meet the learning needs of the Net Generation. Outside of school the Net Gener experiences digital content that is personalized for the learner; in school the Net Gener finds the content delivered in a uniform manner. In the study I conducted, the content being taught was not appropriately paced because it was either too easy or too difficult. Some students mentioned that this was a barrier to learning and disengaged from the class as a result. Typical of this perception, one student explained, "In my typical classroom learning experience, I am often bored because I know most of the material already." Another student characterized how students felt by referring to a photo taken in the classroom: "This picture shows a student staring into space as our teacher is going over easy concepts . . . sometimes we get out of hand and goof off."

More frequently, students mentioned that they found the material too difficult for them to understand. Oftentimes these students mentioned that the reading level of the textbook was beyond their level of competency. As one student pointed out: "When the vocabulary is beyond the understanding of the students, the textbook makes things boring because we have to read everything and it's hard to remember all the things we've read. The textbooks don't even seem interesting because they make it all in their words and we can't understand everything."

Another student explained, "The text book usually explains it in words adults can understand. It uses . . . words that help adults understand better than an average student. Looking at the same repetitive font/information

"This photograph shows a student staring into space as our teacher is going over easy concepts."

everyday tires me." As illustrated by their comments, some students considered inappropriately paced instruction an obstacle to their learning.

Additionally, whereas the Net Generation often interacts with information outside of school using a variety of media that incorporate graphics and video, the Net Generation inside of school gets information presented to them largely auditorily as lectures or as text without the benefits of other supportive media. In my study, the following quote captured the comments of many students and how they perceived information was presented to them in class: "She stands in front of the class and talks and talks . . . I mean they tell us that but she isn't explaining anything she's only talking and going 'BLAH BLAH BLAH' and expects us to understand and know everything."

Another typical complaint by students was the lack of interactivity of information in the classroom. Typical of this comment, one student wrote: "The only interaction that happens during the course of the day is the teacher writing on the white board as you stare at the back of her head trying to hear the soft mumbles over the distractions throughout the room."

Even as the Net Generation has been nurtured in an environment where digital information technologies personalize their learning, pace their education, provide visually rich environments, and create opportunities for interaction, Net Generation students have found information taught auditorily and institutionally in schools. These strategies meet neither their needs nor their expectations for learning, and it should not be surprising that one-third of all students drop out of high school.

Belonging and Collaboration in Schools

Even though the Net Generation has been raised in a collaborative environment, oftentimes networking with others to solve problems at home, students get little opportunity for collaboration or discussion at school despite the evidence that these methods engage students and increase scholastic achievement. Research suggests that only 1% of instruction time is devoted to group work. In the My So-Called Digital Life study that I conducted, many students reported making connections with others, which built a sense of belonging through extracurricular activities such as athletics, band, and theater. However, with the exception of the magnet schools in the study and classes for the gifted and talented, most students perceived they did not have opportunities in class for joint participation in which to apply, analyze, or evaluate information, concepts, and ideas. This perception is aligned with other aforementioned research.

This lack of collaborative opportunities during classroom learning appears to be especially alienating to at-risk students. A typical comment was, "Often I feel like I am all alone and there is nobody around that understands me, at least nobody my age. I often find myself alone at times when everyone else is with friends." Some of these students described alienation from their teacher as contributing to their disengagement from learning. One student confessed that: "Being this tired and as lazy to not even open a te[x]t book makes speaking out another difficult task. Being shy and lazy is a horrible combination. Most of the time my teachers do not even notice I am there. When you are as shy as I am in a classroom full of peers, you don't want to bring more attention to yourself so your questions remain unanswered and forgotten."

During the interviews, low-achieving students expressed that much of the time they were unable to understand the content being covered in the class. Additionally, several students described feeling alone in a subject area that they perceived others understood, while they were still struggling to learn the content. One student wrote: "In most of my classes there are many students that pretty much know everything that is going on so I feel left out because sometimes I don't know what's happening." Another student characterized his experience as follows: "My experience in the classroom is not so good because I'm always lagging. It's like that because I just don't understand the meaning of the teachings." These students felt that they were alone in their ignorance on a particular topic and felt further alienation as they perceived other, more capable students successfully completing the work and answering questions that they were unable to.

When students indicated they felt isolated from other students and teachers, those students who felt alienated overwhelmingly described disengaging from learning. As one student wrote, "They are not a student but they're a student number. This is my experience in the school system. There is an abundance of apathy that seeps into life. It [learning] is a chore." This is consistent with the research from the National Dropout Prevention Center and Network, which has found that alienation is the largest predictor of student dropout; this group of low-achieving students, therefore, should be considered further at risk of dropping out because of their sense of isolation.

Technology in Schools

In the area of technology, the Net Generation has access to a wide range of information and communication technology at home, but most students do not have access to computer learning technology at school. Only a small number of students in my study communicated that computers were part of their typical experience. Usually, when students did mention in-school access to computers they reported using them during technology classes for activities such as learning computer applications, web design, programming, or computer repair. One student wrote: "In this class, we learn about different computer programs. Since this is a class where we learn how to use different computer programs, we have a lot of computers in this room. You can see the teacher helping a student who was having difficulty inserting pictures and text into her website. At the same time, there are students taking notes on what the buttons in Photoshop do."

Whereas some students are using computers to learn about computers, desktop video, digital technologies, and programming, only a small portion of students have access to digital collaboration and information tools in core curricular classes. The findings from this study are further supported by the nationally renowned educational technology researcher Larry Cuban, who found that even with the large investment into computer technology by school districts, only 20% of teachers in K-12 schools integrate computer technologies into the regular academic courses.

Many times when students do have access to technology in school, it is outdated and unreliable. School computers and printers fail frequently, often because there are inadequate technical support systems and insufficient or nonexistent repair technicians. Where many corporations have one technician for every 50 computers, school districts often have one or fewer technicians for every 400 computers. During my study, students often talked about the unreliability of the technology in their classrooms. One student wrote: "With the urgency to get the [work] done, and the problem of one printer, Edward prays that his photo would print." Another student observed, "For every time a gadget saves the day, another frustrates the user into submission."

Other students commented on how outdated the computers were. One student expressed his concerns this way: "It gets me frustrated when I'm not able to get where I need to be because sometimes the computer would start to slow down." Another student noted: "This [school] technology is out of date, poorly made and easily broken. The computers that we have are slow and lack memory. It took me about five attempts and two weeks to load the photograph . . . The computers we use crash more often then bumper cars. I'm almost certain my calculator has more memory than the computers at my school."

CHAPTER 3

STUDENT VOICES

"MIDNIGHT"

It's now tomorrow
And I've been working since yesterday
Somewhere between the research papers
And the literary analysis
I've forgotten what "today" is
So this is high school
And it took me three years of coasting to discover
But I'm finally here
And my brain isn't working
But I'm wide awake
My computer screen dims as my thoughts turn astray
I've never felt more alive in my life
So this is high school
This is the pain and the pleasure
The lethargy and the partial paralysis
The apathy and the ecstasy
It's all the backbreaking work that doesn't pay off
Until you're thirty years old in the suburbs
And waiting for death
The day you finally understand everything,
You're no longer their problem
They kick you to the curb

With a happy handshake and a stern "Start over"
So this is high school.
I think I'm going to like it here . . .

—Ryan McCue

In 2003, I worked on a quantitative study with Dr. Joan Bissel and doctoral student Crista Copp examining student achievement. During the study, I compiled thousands of scores from millions of kids that presented a bleak picture of K-12 education. The statistics of dropping test scores, especially of our high school students, left me numb; I remember feeling confused about the findings. Even though the results were clear about how low our students had scored, I was left wondering why students were performing poorly and disengaging from learning. Why was it that one out of every three students dropped out of high school?

Fortunately, I had another experience that helped me refocus my effort. I was attending a workshop that featured keynote speaker Rick Smolan, the creator of *America 24/7*, part of the *A Day in the Life* series of photography books. The workshop started in darkness. Photographs began to sharpen on a large screen that covered the stage. On a rock, surrounded by green grass and shadowed trees, a little girl stood barefoot on her mud-splattered tiptoes. The picture faded and another photo appeared of a man, high above New York City, precariously perched on an art deco masterpiece, dangling from the top of the building, changing a light bulb. One slide dissolved, and another replaced it.

After the show was finished, Rick Smolan took center stage and spoke of how this project began. He said he was tired of hearing how the world thought of America with disdain, and he was weary of the images that the news media showed of his community. He decided that he wanted to tell his story—the story of how he experienced America. He proceeded to organize 1,000 professional photographers and asked people across the nation to shoot and send him photographs of their experiences. He and his team reflected on those photos, gathered a group of colleagues, and created the photography project that would become the book *America 24/7*.

At hearing this story, I experienced the numbing feeling I had been carrying dissolve into excitement as it struck me that our youth needed an opportunity to voice their story through photographs, captions, and narratives about their school experience. Through their words and images, they might be empowered, as Rick Smolan was in the telling of his story. By getting a voice in their education they might rediscover the shared human experience of their youth and reconnect with a community of parents, educators, policymakers, and professionals who might be able to awaken their aspirations. Furthermore, I hoped that I might get some insight into whether our students perceived schools as places of alienation or communities of support—for which students and at what times? What barriers were our kids encountering in their school experience, and why were they disengaging and dropping out? I wanted to know not only as a researcher but also as an educator and, ultimately, as a father so that I might help my own son and daughter aspire to their American Dream.

From my workshop experience, I coordinated a collaborative project with educators from California State University, Pomona; California Technology Assistance Project, Region 11; and the Covina Valley Unified School District to create the project and book *My So-Called Digital Life*. Two thousand students from 30 middle schools and high schools across the state were given digital cameras and asked to document, in photographs and words, their day-to-day worlds. These schools ranged from Avalon, a school that served students from kindergarten through twelfth grade on Catalina Island, to the Phoenix Academy, a program for students with substance abuse problems. Students from the inner cities to rural parts of the state were able to participate in the project and share their experiences in the book *My So-Called Digital Life*.

From this project, I did an in-depth qualitative study of 120 students (four from each school—two boys and two girls, representing students of different achievement levels). Because the photographs were taken by the students themselves as they worked to capture their perceptions digitally, I could examine the raw and authentic experiences of our kids. Photographs can capture thoughts, feelings, and attitudes beyond the conscious control of the person behind the camera thus providing students with a "photo voice." From those photographs, I was able to interview students about their schooling experience, a subject in which they were the experts. As the educational researcher Gary Anderson of New York University wrote, "Children are experts on their own lives." This combination of data provided the basis for understanding students' perceptions of their learning experiences, which I trust you will find as engaging and helpful as I did for the purposes of re-creating again the best educational system in the world.

In the study, I examined the ways in which students engaged in learning in middle and high school. Additionally, I analyzed the precursors to student disengagement. From the data, three themes emerged: (1) students decide whether to engage in learning based on its perceived value; (2) personalized learning supports students; and (3) students perceive identifiable barriers to their learning.

Perceived Value

In terms of the first theme, students characterized learning activities— and therefore their perceived value—based on three things: utilitarian importance to the students' future, significance or relevance to their current life, and interest value. The merit of each activity was considered in light of its perceived drawbacks, for example, boredom, discomfort, and the effort level. If students felt that the benefits of a learning activity were greater than the drawbacks, students decided to engage. However, if drawbacks outweighed the perceived advantages of the activity, then students chose not to engage.

Future Utilitarian Purpose

Many students expressed that knowledge they will be able to use later in life is valuable and worth their effort and attention. These students, who talked about attending college, saw the skills and processes learned in school as important for their success at the university. Typical of this perspective, one student articulated, "Learning in the classroom is dependent on motivation. For example, a student who's [sic] main concern is getting into a good college, wants to do well in school. Students that

This is how a typical student divides the class into those who work hard and will succeed and those who are "slacking off."

want to get a higher education at college make sure that they learn all that they can in the classroom."

Another student described an example of how differences in motivation are usually displayed in the atmosphere of the classroom.

> This picture simulates what usually goes on in one of my classes. One can easily separate the students in the picture into two groups. The first group, which is easy to locate, are the ones who are hard at work in their desks. These are the ones who will succeed in life, getting a good job and having little to worry about in their futures. The second group is the ones who are talking, and slacking off. These will have a harder time getting through life, and have much more to worry about in their futures. They will sooner or later learn that in order for them to succeed, they are going to have to work harder.

While high-achieving students often expressed a connection between what they were learning and its impact on their future, low-achieving students did not. This disconnect between what they were learning in the classroom and its possible impact on their future education and profession points to why some students fail to engage in learning.

Weighing Current Importance

In addition to considering future benefit, many students expressed that how class curriculum related to their current life was valuable. Many students asserted that the material taught in class needed to have a recognizable purpose and a connection to their life. A student typified this perception when he wrote: "Teachers help to relate content to students' life. Class discussions and projects interest me in learning. I am especially motivated when a teacher tries to explain how the material relates to us." One articulate student went further, writing, "We must practice and utilize what we are taught, which will in turn give us more insight in what we already know. For teenagers, what is being taught must have relevancy and a purpose." Very few students expressed the ability to determine the relevance of content on their own. For instance, one student wrote that he was "[l]istening to the teacher, taking notes, and trying to apply what I am learning to my life."

Whereas students expressed that activities they perceived as meaningful stimulated their engagement, they conveyed that learning experiences they thought were meaningless discouraged student engagement. Many students mentioned becoming apathetic, and even high-achieving students often described their effort and attention to the activity as minimal. When students found the activity meaningless, most students failed to find the reward of an A grade or the threat of an F grade sufficient to warrant engagement in the activity. Based on the findings from the 2005 study by the United States Department of Education suggesting that students who drop out cite irrelevant coursework as their primary reason, some high school students might not perceive graduation as valuable enough for them to continue participating in school. Those students who identify the pointlessness of school activities are likely to be the students who disengage from school and are at higher risk of dropping out.

Weighing Interest

Some students mentioned that learning activities that provided them with an opportunity to hone an area of perceived strength interested them. One student who characterized this perception wrote: "Depending on what the subject is, I like that I'm good at it. For example, I'm really

"With a paintbrush in my hand, I can explore the depths of my creativity."

good with algebra, so I like that class. I really enjoy reading, and I'm good with grammar, so I like English, too." Other students expressed that the value of a learning activity increased if they were able to do something that others were unable to do. An example of a typical response, one student revealed, "Another thing that I find interesting is in math where there is a problem where no one can seem to solve and you have to go through a technical process to find it out is sometimes appealing to me." Students expressed that when they considered themselves to be good in a particular subject, the value of that subject was also high. Furthermore, as students perceived that they were competent in an area or were increasing in competency in an area, they expressed a willingness to engage in the learning and construct meaning. This is consistent with the renowned educational researcher Albert Bandura's social learning theory, which suggests self-efficacy (the perception that one is effective in an area) leads to high student engagement and, ultimately, achievement in an area.

One activity that some students identified as worthwhile was artistic expression. When these students were able to explore their creativity through art, some students perceived this as interesting. One student professed that "[i]t is almost as if, when he takes a paintbrush in his hand, he can explore the depths of his creativity. His happy expression inclines an air of motivation as well."

Another student confirmed this sentiment, writing: "In art you can always express yourself and take out you're [sic] feelings with a painting." Even though all the students who wrote about expressing themselves in art found it valuable, few students wrote about art as a typical experience in their education.

In contrast to the categories such as artistic expression that interested students, there were categories of learning activities such as note taking, lecturing, and reading textbooks that disinterested most students. These students perceived that copying notes was a futile exercise, without purpose, because the teacher could have the notes copied and handed out without asking them to rewrite the exercises. "The teachers normally have the notes typed out, why don't they just make copies and not waste the student's time by making them copy the notes by hand." When most students found an activity meaningless and without interaction, they predominately expressed being disinterested in the activity. Most students did not consider the lectures they heard in class interesting. One typical comment was: "My experience in Classroom learning is Boring because every day the teacher stands at the front of the classroom or walks around the class and talks and talks." Another student expressed that the lecture lacked student interaction and characterized it as follows: "The only interaction that happens during the course of the day is the teacher writing on the white board as you stare at the back of her head trying to hear the soft mumbles over the distractions throughout the room."

A few students described how the teacher became frustrated during the lecture and began to chastise the students. When teachers yelled, some of the students expressed disinterest in the learning. One student provided the following description: "She stands in front of the class and talks and talks and then when kids are talking then the teacher starts

In this photograph, a student expresses her thoughts on school.

yelling at us and tell us 'HOW ARE U GUYS EVER GOING TO LEARN IF YOU NEVER LISTEN?'"

Some students characterized lectures as damaging to the learning process and their level of self-efficacy. One student wrote about the experience this way: "Day in, day out; student[s] tread on these fallacies as they sit-out a lecture. They begin to question themselves, their abilities and potentials."

In addition to the lectures and note taking, the use of textbooks to find answers disinterested most students because it was perceived as meaningless. Typical of this expression, one student wrote: "Who wants to spend hours finding answers out of the text and just copying it down? It has already been written—why write it again?" Another student commented, "When teachers only teach what is in the textbooks, it has the tendency to loose [sic] a student's attention and desire to learn."

Even though students found the reading of chapters from a textbook a predominate form of learning in the classroom, many students did not find this method an effective means of teaching and learning. Many students became bored in the learning activity when it consisted primarily of reading and answering questions from the textbook because they saw little value in summarizing the information from books onto worksheets. Some students expressed that the futile learning environment was disheartening. For instance, a highly articulate student wrote: "Countless examples could be brought up of that enthusiastic spark disintegrating. And truly there is often no point in learning materials presented in books and worksheets. Many conclude lessons as fronts, illusions of achievements. Facts are to be learned as facts, applications aren't usually required. Necessary experience isn't gained, proving the results fruitless."

As illustrated in the aforementioned examples, many students framed their experience of learning in the context of its meaning or meaninglessness; and in many cases this context was a precursor to whether they became interested or disinterested.

Weighing Perceived Value vs. Drawbacks

If students found that their level of boredom from a learning activity outweighed the activity's potential benefits for their future or its relevance to their current lives, most students mentioned disengaging completely.

Typical of this consideration, one student first expressed the importance of school by articulating, "Being involved with school and learning there helps enrich your mind with things that you'll use later in life." However, later, when the same student perceived the learning as boring, he expressed the following: "My attitude would try to be enthusiastic, but the fact that I'm doing something not exciting would discourage my enthusiasm. Instead of getting a good result, it's just another boring lesson. The fact that I have to listen/read another boring lesson, would just make my thoughts drift away." Even those students who perceived school as important to their future often disengaged from learning when the drawbacks outweighed the perceived benefits.

When students perceived that the learning was not relevant, beneficial, or valuable, many expressed deciding to engage in other cognitive activities. One student commented, "I have often found myself dosing [sic] off or starring [sic] at fellow classmates giggling about some sort of entertainment hidden by text books. During these long, exhausting days, it's hard to think about education or any means of research or just doing work."

Another student added, "They are listening to a lecture by the teacher who is at the front of the classroom. Some of the students are looking at other things. Some students are concentrating on their friends and are talking to them. Others are looking at the front bored and uninterested."

An additional student also mentioned that "[o]thers are looking at the front bored and uninterested."

Other students wrote about disconnecting from learning by using personal technologies such as CD players, iPods, and cell phones. For example, in reference to the photograph below one student revealed that

> students doze off, spend [h]ours listening to I-pods, or just daydreaming until you have an absolute blank stair [sic] on your face. Some more than others, but we can all confess we have done it. As my years in school I feel like it is getting worse as the years go on. In the photograph that I

A student disengages from learning while listening to his iPod.

took, there was a student who is changing the songs on his iPod while the teacher was trying to teach his lesson. If I was one of the persons in the photograph I would probably be listening to my mp3 player and would have no idea what the teacher is talking about. Some of my teachers make class so boring it is very hard to pay attention. I know the teachers aren't there to entertain us but it would be nice for the teachers to make class a little more interesting.

As illustrated in the aforementioned examples, many students who mentioned becoming disinterested in the learning activity also expressed subsequently engaging in other cognitive activity. The findings from the study suggest students are continuously negotiating the meaning and value of every classroom activity. Many students described choosing to engage or disengage through a process of measuring the proposed value of the activity against its drawbacks, such as boredom and alienation.

These findings are consistent with the USC educational researcher Richard Clark's model of motivation which suggests that there are three types of values that increase the likelihood of engagement in an activity: 1) utility (an activity beneficial to the person); 2) interest (an activity that has intrinsic appeal to the person); and 3) importance (an activity that increases the level of competence in the person). When all three values are present, student engagement is more likely; however, if any of the three is missing, goal pursuit is less likely. This model supports the findings that suggest that even though some students perceived the activity beneficial to their future career or college education, these students still became disinterested in the activity. These students also need to feel that what they're learning is intrinsically appealing and potentially important for increasing their level of competence before choosing to engage. Most students mentioned that the values and meaning they placed on the learning activity were a precursor to whether they chose to engage. For those activities that students do not consider valuable, students largely expressed disengaging from learning regardless of its negative impact on their grade.

Personalized Learning

In the first theme, students talked about their perception of the value of the learning activity affecting the extent to which they decided to engage in the activity. In this second theme, students expressed that when personalized supports were present in the academic environment, they believed the supports enabled them to persist in their learning. When these students were able to personalize their education by applying concepts to their life, customizing their environment, or building their own meaning, students perceived the learning context or setting to be supportive and were willing to remain engaged in their involvement in a task despite feeling initially confused, frustrated, or angry. As generalized concepts and areas of study are personalized, many students expressed being able to construct meaning based on past knowledge, experiences, and values.

Teacher Supports to Learning

Many students mentioned that they viewed teachers who were able to personalize learning for their specific needs as supportive. For instance, some students regarded teachers' use of oral storytelling as helpful to them in making meaning out of the facts and information presented. A typical comment was: "What I enjoy about my favorite class, Spanish, is that our teacher, Ms. Fernandez, almost always has a story that relates to what she is teaching and I really have fun hearing her stories and the stories sometimes help me better understand what she is teaching."

A few students also mentioned the positive affective responses from teachers as helpful. These students expressed that if the teachers made them laugh, they would focus more intently on the material being presented. One student communicated, "In our typical learning environment in this class, we are usually paying attention to Ms. Rodriguez's lesson and sometimes we have a laugh or two." Many students mentioned that when they were enjoying the class, this helped them to stay involved.

Several students also expressed that when teachers encouraged student interaction and involvement, this was helpful to them. This interaction included asking students questions and assisting students one-on-one.

One student remarked, "My teachers try to get us as involved as possible and make sure that we know what is going on and understand the material." Many students perceived that teachers were supporting them when the instructor corrected them in a one-on-one context. One student explained that, "The photograph that I selected communicated a lot of my learning experience because every time someone has a problem or [is] having a hard time understanding the work that the teacher gave you, of course you need to ask for help. Otherwise you will never learn anything if you are not corrected by your teacher."

A few students mentioned that when they were given individual assistance they not only viewed this assistance as supportive but also felt grateful to their teachers. "If i [sic] were this student then in my head I'll probably be saying 'ok I kind of get it' . . . I will also be asking for some help for every step. I will also be thanking the teacher that had helped me on my work."

The aforementioned students identified teachers' storytelling, interaction, and one-on-one support as helpful because the student was able to understand the content covered in the class. When these students were then able to apply the content within the context of their own life experiences, they expressed a willingness to engage in the learning. Many students perceived that the role of the teacher to help create connections between the material of the lesson and their own lives was critical to them. Students expressed that teachers specifically interested and engaged them when they told stories, provided relevant examples, and applied the content to their future life.

Collaborative Learning

In addition to the perception that teacher support is helpful, students considered peer assistance as another aid to personalize their education. Within the context of collaborative learning, students felt supported when they were able to ask group members for help on particular questions. Some students expressed that because teachers may be too busy to answer questions during class, small groups enabled students to get more immediate feedback and assistance. One student commented, "I enjoy working in groups because you can ask your fellow classmates for help in case the teacher is busy helping another student." Additionally, many students mentioned that the interaction and exchange of viewpoints in collaborative groups helped them to solve problems together, without the help of an adult. One student asserted, "Working with people is more interesting when we use OUR brains to figure it out."

As illustrated in the examples, collaborating groups that included more capable peers helped many students to understand concepts that individually they were unable to comprehend. Some students found the help from their peers more accessible than the support from a single teacher who might have been assisting other students. This is consistent with Vygotsky's Zone of Proximal Development, whereby students' understanding can be extended through the assistance of more advanced students.

Customizing Information and the Environment

Most students perceived the ability to customize the learning environment to be important. Furthermore, technology helped them personalize their workspace. One student explained how students can decorate their work area to reflect their personality: "We are allowed to tailor our stations to our own specific needs and interests. If my interest is Music, I can load all of the music editing and mixing software to produce and burn my own original hiphop beats to CD. If it is Math, I can specialize my station with all of the latest mind bending math equation mazes and games. So, in short, the photograph portrays us at our personalized cyberstations."

Several students conveyed that the support provided by technology extended beyond computers and included the ability to use other media, such as music, to inspire them as they worked on individual assignments. For instance, one student observed that "there are always some students who need an extra little bit of inspiration to get their work done. Now that we have things like cd players and headphones some students use them while they are in class . . . music can truly be the inspiration needed to concentrate better in class."

In addition to tailoring their personal environment, students perceived the on-demand access to information, assignments, and resources as helpful. Students communicated that direct access to information both in the classroom and outside the normal context of the classroom was helpful in overcoming personal limitations. As one student explained, this accessibility was convenient "when I have forgotten my assignment entirely or I wasn't at school that day. I can use the internet and go on a school site to find out what my assignment was. The internet helps me pay attention."

Multimedia Examples

In addition to the increased access to resources and information that computers provided, many students expressed that multimedia technologies and visuals helped provide concrete examples to abstract concepts. A variety of visual media examples provided help to students in comprehending the curriculum. In one typical example, a student described the various learning aids available in the classroom:

> Posters on the walls with tips, video, overhead . . . The posters on the wall always have something to do with that particular class. They always have tips to help you in your work. It's supposed to have you see your work easier because of the tips the posters are giving. They also have at least one computar to either help the teachers with records or for students to use when needed. They also have one T.V. in the room just in case the teachers need to view something related to the subject on video. The typical classrooms are always using an overhead to view things bigger on the wall so the whole class can see. . . . The overhead is used to enlarge something on the wall so it can be viewed for even students in the back.

A few students mentioned the visuals provided in PowerPoint helping to promote their learning, as this student intimated: "The teacher helps her students and gets them involved with her work. She likes explaining things visually by showing them powerpoints so it is easier for them to comprehend. It also shows the students excited and ready to learn."

Beyond the support that the visuals provided, a few students perceived teaching aids that promoted auditory learning were helpful. One of these students observed that

> finding out which study technique helps them to learn best can really motivate some students to study on their own. For instance, my humanities teachers let us listen to different types of music including classical, baroque and romantic music to make us more aware of how they reflect the changing lifestyle of the people in the different time periods. My Spanish teacher did a similar thing where she let us listen to a Spanish pop song and told us to write the lyrics down so that we can both practice listening to the words, understand their meaning and know how to spell them out.

These students illustrate that the use of technology and multimedia can provide illustrations and examples of abstract concepts that help many of them to learn. Some students also conveyed that the computer allowed them to personalize their virtual environment through the selection of preferred colors, music, fonts, and graphics that were meaningful to them. Through these tools students contextualized general concepts into specific media examples that illustrated those concepts.

Perceived Barriers

The following section examines the third theme, that students perceive barriers to classroom learning. Some students expressed that there were instructional, personal, and social barriers to classroom learning. Some students perceived that they already knew the material and the slow pace of the instruction presented a barrier to learning. Other students mentioned personal limitations or feelings of alienation as obstacles to learning.

Personal Issues

Beyond mentioning the pacing or feelings of alienation as cause for disengagement, which I've touched on before, a few students described becoming disinterested in learning because of their own personal problems, such as poor eyesight, shyness, the death of a family member, and sleepiness. One student divulged, "It's like that because I just don't understand the meaning of the teachings. Sometimes it's my eyes I don't have great eyes sometimes they're good or sometimes they messed up and that's one of the reasons I do bad. I get frustrated not seeing very well."

Another student shared that he became disinterested in learning and prone to behavior problems after the death of his father. "I used to skip school with my friends to go to my house. I used to have problems with my anger, I used to make a big deal . . . [around] the principal, the administrators, teachers I didn't even know, I used to make a lot of drama. That [is] how come I had problems. I couldn't handle my father's death. That's why I was the way I was."

This girl persists in learning even when confronted with confusion.

Differences Between Boys and Girls

When some boys failed to understand the material, they expressed feeling angry regardless of their achievement levels. One low-achieving student identified with another student's feelings of anger by writing: "At first he feels a bit mad because the teacher is telling him he is wrong, but then he starts to understand that the teacher is just trying to help him excel in his algebra."

A high-achieving student characterized this anger when he explained, "When the student cannot figure something out, fury rises up in them and the first thing that comes out is 'I hate school!' I believe that that is the reason why there is a negative attitude towards school."

Some boys also expressed anger when they were not being acknowledged or when they did not have a voice in the group. One boy fumed, "I'm really mad. No one is listening to my idea. They are too wrapped up in themselves and self-centered and no one takes any time to just listen to everybody and put them together to make the ultimate idea."

Whereas some boys expressed anger when they failed to understand or be heard, many girls expressed their lack of understanding as confusion or frustration. The only comment by a girl in which anger was mentioned was in response to the teacher's anger at the student. However it was typical for girls to mention confusion or frustration. For instance, one girl described that "[i]n this picture I was trying to portray how I see myself in computer class. The look that the student has is an interested look yet confused, she's not sure what to do but she is willing to learn."

Another girl, relating her own experience to a female classmate, wrote: "Francesca raises her hand to ask about a question she was confused on." However, when most mid- and high-achieving girls did not know the answer to a question or felt confused, most of them also talked about persisting in the activity. One girl wrote that "[t]he teacher asked [a question]. She opened the book. What is that word again. I need to find that page."

Based on the findings, there are patterns in the differences in how girls and boys react when they fail to understand content in class.

Despite these differences, however, there were three themes that emerged from the data common to both boys and girls. First, when learning was perceived as valuable for its utilitarian purpose to assist students in their future, for its natural interest, or for its importance and relevance to their lives, students were willing to engage in the learning. Second, when students were able to personalize the learning to support their education, students were more inclined to persist in the activity. Finally, when students became disinterested in learning, rather than participating in academic activities, they engaged in alternative cognitive pursuits such as sleeping and daydreaming. These distracted states often arose in isolated educational environments in which students perceived instructors unwilling to help. When these conditions were present, students expressed feeling a range of emotions from anger and confusion, to frustration and boredom. Students conveyed that the negativity that these emotions created in the educational environment were precursors to their disengagement.

CHAPTER 4

MY SO-CALLED
DIGITAL LIFE

INSTRUCTIONAL TECHNOLOGY is a powerful way to engage students and increase participation in collaborative learning in a variety of social contexts important for student learning. One type of instructional technology that engages students in discussion and creates a sense of inclusion is Computer Supported Collaborative Learning (CSCL). CSCL is a system of collaborative learning that uses technology to build knowledge and expertise, support student learning, and facilitate group interaction As a result, student engagement and achievement are likely to be enhanced. Students use the digital tools to dialogue with other group members and to create connections between abstract concepts and media objects.

Despite the effectiveness of the application only a small number of new applications have been developed. One such application, the Emaze Simulation, was developed by a team of us at Covina Valley Unified School District in 2001 and piloted at a smaller level within the district. In 2005, we implemented it in 30 secondary classrooms across the state. The Emaze Simulation involved a series of standards-based learning activities designed to build student knowledge through an inquiry-based process using email exchanges with community experts, who included professional photographers, writers, and researchers. In the following section, you will get a sense of what students thought, felt, and learned within the Emaze Simulation.

The Student Emaze Experience

When students described the types of activities they typically experienced in the CSCL project, most students characterized the activities as centering on the use of the computer to email, take photographs, and write narratives based on the language arts state standards. Referring to the photograph on the following page, one student wrote: "This picture was taken by my friend while I was typing my narrative for the emaze solutions project. This represents my learning experience during the emaze solutions project, because during this project we were constantly on the computer. During this project I did more things on the computer than I had before. During this project I typed many things on the computer at school than I did before. Usually I would just go on the computer sometimes during school, but for this project I used the computer almost every day."

Students such as this one commented that, through their experience with the digital camera and writing, they learned about the life of other students and about education in other schools because there were students from diverse classrooms, from schools that were located on an island (Catalina), and from urban and suburban schools as well. One student expressed that after exchanging photographs and reading the blogs, "I am now aware that there are other people who did this project that have the same ideas and beliefs about different subjects and schools."

After taking photographs, students shared and discussed their experiences of learning as captured by the photographs with other members and then posted their photographs online so students from other participating schools could view them. One student characterized the Emaze experience this way: "In this picture you can also see that three people, such as these girls, can have fun with technology. They are showing each other their pictures." In addition to sharing their photographs with other students, each student posted their photographs online for their professional photographer mentor to view and provide feedback. This sharing with the professional was portrayed by a student who stated, "It might not be one of the best picture[s] but it shows the comments from the [professional] photographer, and the photographer's pictures. . . ."

A student uses the computer while participating in the CSCL project.

After capturing the photographs, students reflected on them by answering questions and sharing their responses and feedback with other students online. Some students commented on this peer collaboration aspect of the project. A typical comment was the following: "If I was the person in this photo I would be working with the computer. I would be enjoying myself with this project and I'm about to write down answers to the project because I'm a research person too."

Some students commented on the experience of writing that was pervasive through this project. One student mentioned, "We had to write the six paragraphs for the chosen photographs. Students were very busy trying to finish everything. They had to choose their six photos to write their paragraphs." Another student remarked, "During this project I typed many things on the computer at school than I did before. Usually I would just go on the computer sometimes during school, but for this project I used the computer almost every day. The picture shows me writing the narrative for the emaze solutions project."

Influence on Perception of Engagement: CSCL Themes

Examination of the CSCL data revealed that there were five themes that emerged to address the question: What were the ways in which students' perception of engagement were influenced in a CSCL experience? These five themes were: 1) using computers to help; 2) being connected; 3) applying digital know-how; 4) trying their best; and 5) looking at things differently. When students perceived that they were using computers to help, connecting to others who were participating in the project, or applying digital know-how, many students expressed that they began trying their best and looking at things differently. Many students mentioned that the CSCL experience influenced their engagement through the process of providing a sociocultural context of learning with practitioners, supporting their learning, and contextualizing generalized concepts into specific examples. These students suggested that these experiences helped to engage them and that these experiences were antecedents to their willingness to try their best on the learning activities.

Theme One: Using Computers to Help

Among the five themes, using computers to help was the most dominant. Most students expressed that the computers supported their ability to learn by providing opportunities to search for information easily, experience differentiated pacing, access website resources, visualize examples through streaming video, and utilize writing tools. Many students commented on the central nature of the computer in the project as a supportive component to their learning. One articulate student wrote: "This is also to show that the computer is a 'part' of the student body and that without it we would be missing a vital piece in our learning system." Even though other students did not use the body metaphor in their writing about their computer use, most noted the support the computer provided. A typical comment was the following: "Learning has become a lot easier as a result of the technology."

These students are using the computer in an attempt to get help on their own.

Although many of the remarks about computer use were general in nature, some students identified specific ways in which the computer helped them in their learning. Some students commented on the ease at which information could be found on the web. Referencing the photograph below, a student wrote: "I'm the two students in my photograph. I'm probably thinking that using the computer to help me is easier than always asking the teacher for help."

In addition to the ease of finding information, students described how websites and their integration of media helped them better understand the material. One student characterized using the Internet as follows: "The Internet sites gives me knowledge to finish the task at hand. When I'm having trouble with an assignment and I need to help, I sometimes go on the internet to look for useful information pertaining to my task. Other times, I don't know how to proceed further. Thusly, I check the internet for sites that help me better understand what I need to know."

Other students mentioned that the specific media elements on websites, such as photographs and video, helped them comprehend the material by providing examples of the concepts. One student communicated: "It's hard to understand what other people went through. I'd rather see the things happen over the internet by mini-clips posted on the computer. Well, we can't always do something in that way. But if there's enough technology in the class we can do it the technology way. Using the computer gets me information I need and when I need it."

Another student summarized what most students of the CSCL project expressed regarding the support of computers: "Learning has become much easier as a result of the technology that is in the schools. The computer and internet has made research a lot easier, and much more fun."

In addition to acknowledging the support the online CSCL tools provided, some students mentioned that the computer aided in editing work by making it easier to correct. For instance, a student wrote: "I feel it would be easier for me and maybe the students. It would be easier to learn more. It is also neater than writing out a whole essay with smudge marks and erase marks." Another student added, "You can also type things and print them out. It makes things neater."

A few students reflected on how the CSCL tools enabled them to compare their photographs and work with those of peers. Referencing the photograph on the following page, a student described that "there is a laptop that is being used to accomplish various things relating to the Emaze project. The laptop is probably being used to attach photographs to an email that is being submitted. The person using the laptop is probably focused on working on the Emaze project. . . . They may be curious about how their photographs may look compared to others."

As part of the prewriting for the narrative, students were given access to online, graphical organizers to help organize their thoughts into a narrative essay. A few students commented on these organizers. For instance, a student wrote: "Diagrams and notes from [a] computer helps students to understand." Another student observed, "It shows how technical learning has gotten thoughout the years of evolution and progress in technol[o]gy. You can study online notes and diagrams so [you] can understand the subject better."

Another type of help students mentioned the computer provided was in the area of differential pacing. Some students perceived they were

A student uses the computer while participating in the Emaze Project.

able to direct some of their learning and move at their own pace. One student noticed that "[t]he biggest difference is that in the typical learning experience the class moves together, but in the emaze solution experience we were able to move at our own pace." Another student mentioned, "We move at our own rate."

Students also expressed that the access to the digital camera gave them choices about what they wanted to do. One student reported, "In the Emaze Solution project, they [students] are using cameras, they are not in a classroom, they are doing what they want to, and they look very interested in what they are doing."

The digital cameras allowed the learning to occur outside the regular confines of the classroom and extended the opportunity for learning into their own homes, as described by this student: "In my photograph there is the emaze project screen on a laptop. This project was enjoyable especially when we got to take the digital camera home. I had a lot of fun with the camera. I was glad that we got to use a digital camera instead

Students use a digital camera to capture exactly what they want.

of a film camera. This project . . . gave me a lot of experience with the art of photographs."

Because the media choices gave students various opportunities to understand the material in different ways, students persisted in their learning, as demonstrated by those students who worked at home and after school on the project, and expressed determination in finishing and in giving their best on the activities despite stress and initial frustration.

Other ways the computer assisted the student was by supporting the use of the digital photographs, word processors, and online graphical organizers in narrative writing. The digital images gave many students a concrete way to begin sharing abstract ideas, feelings, or perceptions in their blogs, expository paragraphs, and, eventually, narrative essays. Most students incorporated their photographs into their writings and invited others to interact with them, using the photograph as an impetus for writing. Other tools, such as the word processor, made editing easy for students, and the online graphical program enabled students to organize their ideas, thus assisting students in writing. All of these CSCL supports were ways in which student engagement was influenced.

Theme Two: Being Connected

The second strong theme that emerged was being connected. Students described how the CSCL project established a community that strengthened over the length of the program. Through the project, students expressed developing connections with other students, teachers, photographers, scholars, and writers. Through these bonds, students mentioned beginning to identify themselves as members of the My So-Called Digital Life group (also known as the Emaze Solutions group), whose membership was dependent on their participation. This membership contributed to students' willingness to engage even when activities became stressful and difficult. The desire to be affiliated with the group positively influenced their engagement in the project. By being connected to a larger circle of people, many students mentioned that it influenced their engagement in the academic activities as they underwent an active social process of learning. Through the social interactions, students acquired and contributed to the beliefs, behaviors, and ideas of the community. Initial involvement was encouraged as other more active members invited newcomers to participate.

Typical of such a sense of connection, one student group wrote: "There are students in all of our pictures which shows that we are all connected through this emaze project." Among the students, most expressed that this feeling of shared involvement extended beyond their immediate class and included students from other schools. One student remarked, "I'm part of a community because I am know [sic] aware that there are other people who did this project that have the same ideas and beliefs about different subjects about school. In a way I also feel connected to the other people who were part of this project in other schools, even though I don't know them. You can spend years in a community and never get to know them. You know they are there, whether you see them or not. If you're lucky, you actually get to meet and know some of these people."

Three girls share their photographs on the computer.

This sense of connection occurred in conjunction with the sharing of ideas, thoughts, and photographs in blogs, emails, and small groups. One student wrote: "This photograph was taken during the last days of the Emaze Solution Project. In this picture you can also see that three people, such as these girls, can have fun with technology. They are showing each other their pictures. Three of the girls are sharing their pictures with each other."

Many students perceived that the photographs provided them with a way to visually express their underlying thoughts. One student commented, "Taking pictures is the total emaze learning experience. Showing the types of learning opposed to talking about it is always better. Being able to express your thoughts, feeling and beliefs about school through pictures is wonderful."

Additionally, many students expressed that the visual aspects of the project, such as the streaming video that could be accessed through websites, provided a way to better understand other people. Students emphasized again and again that the visual shared references in the photographs and streaming video were important to them.

Many students perceived that, through this sharing, they were able to learn about each other, which in turn encouraged the development of additional connections. Many students expressed a sense of curiosity and interest when learning from their fellow students. For instance, one student wrote: "Our lives changed a bit because we get to look into the lives of other students not just yours which is also very exciting." For some students, the academic online interaction developed into a bond of friendship, as illustrated by this student comment: "I have made various new friends which is cool, also I know more about our friendly community, Covina!"

Additionally, many students began to associate themselves with the larger membership of practitioners, including professional photographers, scholars, and graduate students. Some students mentioned an affiliation with this group of scholars after interacting with them through the computer. One student remarked, "The Enter key opens a whole new experience for a student such as myself, to become a computer educated scholar." However, a more common affiliation occurred between the students and the professional photographers. One student characterized this connection to the profession this way: "I'm hoping to become a photographer as a career, I guess you can say doing the emaze project was a sort of inspiration." Another student more directly expressed his connection as a "true photographer" when he indicated, "I was always thinking about how I could get a picture from the different things going on around school. I feel like by doing that, that I was a true photographer and felt like my pictures came out really nice. I was always coming up with new ideas and shots."

Another girl commented, "I think that I now qualify to belong to the brotherhood of professional photographers and impact my world with powerful images." Through this Emaze Simulation, many students enculturated the norms (e.g., using the rule of thirds when taking a photograph), values (e.g., seeing the world differently), products (e.g., digital photographs, captions), and tools of the professionals (e.g., digital camera, Polaroid cache).

Theme Three: Applying Digital Know-How

The third theme that emerged was applying digital know-how. Students perceived that through their newly acquired writing and photography skills, along with the opportunity to present their work to an authentic audience through the publication of their work in a book (*My*

So-Called Digital Life) that would be distributed to bookstores nationwide, they were able to apply their learning in the outside world. Many students commented that the project enabled them to teach and help others through their written and photographed experiences. These students perceived that by sharing their experiences they were helping other students and even the larger community of adults understand how to improve schools.

Many students commented on the importance of producing work for an authentic audience. These students knew that an audience of other students, photographers, graduate students, community members, and teachers would be viewing their work. One student affirmed the distinctive impact an authentic audience can have on the academic environment: "Yes, there is a big difference. This was not like normal school. We were able to have digital cameras and use them and take them home. We all got to do this together and we got cameras and people are going to look at our pictures."

Some students understood that because the larger community would be viewing their work, they would be able to help the public look at the issue from a different perspective. For example, one student commented, "There should be more students involved with projects like this because I myself have learned much from this experience and realized how to make the community around us better. If more kids are participating in a project like this then more kids may realize this too and might help out more to make the community around us better. By giving people feedback about this photo project and them taking the advice I give, they are able to fix things by what I had to say and how they can make it better."

Some students reported that the project gave them the opportunity to teach others. One student expressed this commonly held sentiment in this way: "The learning experience from the photo, however, is how I used the camera to capture a moment in time to teach something." Some students recognized that, through this opportunity to instruct others, they were able to effect change in their community as well. "Emaze has taught me that I can become a social agent of change. I think that I can take this information and apply it to issues in my community and become a social agent of change as result of the Emaze Simulation."

Another student expressed how he hoped to effect change by helping others: "I feel that through my photography, I can try to help others make better choices than I have made in my past . . . I feel that it may be possible for me to actually make someone stop and think before heading down the wrong life path. I haven't glamorized our choices or the life I have lived, but only tried to tell the truth and hope that I can stop at least one person from destroying their life."

In addition to the awareness that the application of their new digital know-how would help others, many students felt that the knowledge from the CSCL project would be useful in their own life. One student characterized this understanding as follows: "I will never forget. I can use the things I have learned with my everyday experience. I learned how to tell my story and show my emotion through the lens of a camera." Many students perceived that by utilizing and applying their knowledge, they gained further insights and a sense of purpose. One especially articulate girl noted,

> We must practice and utilize what we are taught, which will in turn give us more insight in what we already know. For teenagers what is being taught must have relevancy and a purpose. Just as students find relevancy and a purpose in hands-on classes I found such in doing the E-maze project. My experience from this project has proven it true. I witnessed my classmates rummaging through the thesaurus at 9:30 on a Friday night to better enhance their narratives in an effort to improve their chances of being chosen. Whether it is doing science labs, painting in art class or just mistakes I've made in the past, I think we learn by doing. In *The Art of Looking Sideways*, Alan Fletcher said, "The fact is that the mind thinks with ideas not information, so acquiring knowledge is useless unless one learns how to use it. A dictionary may contain all the words but no one can tell a poet which to choose or what to write."

Many students perceived the CSCL project as meaningful because they were able to apply their learning by sharing the product of their knowledge (narrative writing, blogs, photographs, and the book) with an authentic audience of members of the group, community members, and adults. These students expressed that the application of the knowledge they gained through the project gave them a sense of purpose in their learning. This finding is consistent with the results from Cohen and Riel's study whereby students achieved at higher rates when they wrote for an authentic audience than when students wrote only for their teacher (1989). By applying generalized knowledge into contextualized works meaningful to the student and by presenting to an authentic audience, students mentioned that their engagement was positively influenced.

Theme Four: Trying Their Best

The fourth theme that emerged was trying their best. Many students expressed how the project inspired them to work to the best of their ability and some even commented on the change in the amount of effort they put into the project versus the amount they typically put into school. For example, when asked if there was a difference in the experience between their first and second photographs (the first denoting a typical school experience and the second, the student's experience during the project), one student expressed: "Definitely there is a difference between the photos. In the first one the students are just sort of blowing off their work and going through the motions. But in the second Emaze photo, the students are doing their best to complete their work to the best of their ability."

Because many of the students found the work challenging, they indicated that it was necessary to give their best. One student confessed, "There were many things I didn't get about technology and had hard times with certain things so I had to try my best." Another reason students mentioned putting forth their best effort was they were excited by the project. A student expressed this commonly held perception as follows: "All of the students have yellow folders close by them. These folders contain all of our assignments and procedures for the Emaze project. I believe that this shows how everyone tried their hardest to complete the project. It also shows that some of the students learning experience during this project was exciting and they were willing to work."

The third reason that some students cited for doing their best was for the sake of others. Some students expressed a sense of interdependence among the group. For instance, one student wrote: "My thought would be 'I want to work hard' so that the rest of the people that are doing the same thing as us could get the best of us." Furthermore, many students mentioned they were willing to persist on the tasks beyond the confines of the classroom. For example, some students were willing to spend voluntary hours in the evening to work on their writings and photographs. "[M]y friends know that now if you stay at school on a Friday night there can be a good reason. I stayed to get my pics submitted and they thought that was crazy. Then they showed up to see me."

Students also described their high level of concentration and persistence in the project. One student commented, "The difference between the two [experiences] is that normally once I exited the classroom I would stop thinking about the class. Now with the Emaze Solution Stimulation project I have been thinking more about school and schoolwork. I've had to try to capture what I was doing in my classes for this project so I was always trying to remember what we did in class. I was non-stop thinking and worrying about my picture taking and how to show my school environment and how I learn."

As students gave their best, they perceived that they substantially improved in their abilities. "It shows that we learned how to shoot good pictures. Both of the people in the photo are taking pictures of different things at different angles. They really look like they are concentrating on taking a good picture." Several students mentioned that this high level of concentration and effort enabled them to advance their studies.

For instance, one of the students wrote: "The photo that I took shows what I learned and what I went through in the Emaze learning atmosphere. Everywhere I go now all I think about is what would that look like if I took a picture of it. Even though I wasn't that great at taking pictures in the beginning, but I tried my best to get my best images and now I have improved alot in my photo taking skills."

Because most of the students perceived the project as exciting, interdependent, and challenging, many of them were willing to persist, concentrate, and, ultimately, give their best effort in the project. This finding contrasted with the findings that suggested that most students in their typical school experience expressed minimal levels of engagement and, in some cases, expressed complete disengagement from learning.

Theme Five: Looking at Things Differently

The final theme to emerge was looking at things differently. Students mentioned that they began to see their community, school, and world differently than they had before the project and that they were able to think and learn differently. Students often commented that the digital camera was a catalyst for seeing the community and school in a new light. One student noted that "walking around with a camera lets you see things you don't really notice before." Another student commented, "Taking pictures of our community let me see things that I had never seen here before."

By the end of the project, many students conveyed they were seeing things they had not noticed previously. Even those items students had previously ignored because they were mundane or ordinary were perceived as worthy of notice. "With this project I was able to view our school like in a slightly different way. I saw many everyday things for the first time!"

Ultimately, many students realized that the CSCL project changed the way they thought about learning. One student remarked, "My typical learning experience is with limited technology, but with this emaze simulation, I have learned about all the different ways of learning with technology, and how it has changed the way students think and learn."

In addition to seeing, thinking, and learning differently, a small subgroup of students reported changed feelings because of the project. One student commented, "In the beginning of the year I would just take a picture and think nothing of it. Now when I take a picture I look at all the different angles and it makes me feel different inside." Another student portrayed this new feeling as a newfound confidence: "Helped me see more and notice more about the community and things around me. I learned about myself and got confidence." As a result of the project many students gained a new perspective towards their school, community, learning, and environment.

The Wisconsin professor James Paul Gee in his book *What Video Games Have to Teach Us about Learning and Literacy* has suggested that one way to determine if active learning has transformed a learner is to understand whether they see and experience a semiotic domain of language, signs, symbols, and artifacts differently. This approach would suggest that students in this study engaged in active learning because they were enculturated into a new affiliation of writers, photographers, and scholars. From engagement with these practitioners, students expressed seeing the world differently.

Similarities of High-, Mid-, and Low-Achieving Groups

Subgroups' Experiences: Enjoyment

Students from all achieving groups expressed an overall enjoyment of the CSCL project. Students found the ability to express themselves through the technology, such as the digital cameras and laptops, engaging. For example, one low-achieving student wrote: "In my photograph, the students are just getting ready to work on their emaze project. They are just getting ready to go to the computer lab and are getting papers handed out. Actually they seem to be in a good mood, because most of the students are talking."

Another low-achieving student commented, "We use laptops in class, and i [sic] think that using laptops in class will help students learning. It is also a lot of fun."

The mid-level-achieving students also expressed a high degree of enjoyment, oftentimes expressed as fun. A typical comment among mid-achieving students was expressed by one student: "Well the amount of work is quite even [between typical classes and this project] but this Emaze Solution project is a bit more fun."

Subgroups' Experiences: Creativity

Many students from all three achievement levels expressed enjoyment in conjunction with the creativity that they were able to express. Some students likened the experience to more creative elective courses, as this representative high-achieving student observed: "With EMAZE we have been able to learn through a creative side that is not often exposed in school unless you are in an art class." A low-achieving student wrote about how this project helped him with the art of photography. "I had a lot of fun with the camera. I was glad that we got to use a digital camera instead of a film camera. This project . . . gave me a lot of experience with the art of photographs."

Subgroups' Experiences: Engagement

Many students at all three achievement levels expressed that, because of their enjoyment, they were willing to concentrate and persist in learning. For instance, a high-achieving student wrote: "if i was the person in this photo i would be working with the computer. i would be enjoying myself with this project and i'm about to write down answers to the project because i'm a research person too." One low-achieving student, observing the intense concentration of her classmate, wrote: "She is determined to finish her research."

A mid-level student characterized this transition from the feeling of excitement to sustained action on their part this way: "There WAS a difference because this was not a normal activity! It was very exciting in the beginning and by the end I was planning out which pictures I would take." Low-achieving students also expressed recognizing this link between enjoyment of the project followed by action of some sort. One low-achieving student wrote that he and his fellow students were in a "good mood" and that "the students were just getting ready to work on their emaze project." Some students expressed they would continue to use the knowledge in their own lives. One student characterized this

These students are concentrating on their CSCL activity.

sentiment as follows: "I believe that I will be able to go from this experience with a lot of knowledge about photography. Through this I will be able to document my family and all of the things that happen to us. I will enjoy making interesting photos with my friends and family."

Subgroups' Experiences: Stress

Despite the enjoyment of the project, some students from all three groups expressed feeling a high level of stress. They attributed the stress to the amount of work as well as to the limited time frame in which they had to complete the project. Additionally, some students commented on the unreliability of the technology, such as printers. High-achieving students expressed this degree of strain more often than either the mid- or low-achieving groups. Seventy-two percent of the students who mentioned increased anxiety because of the project were high achieving as compared to only 28% of the mid- and low-achieving students. One high-achieving student characterized the amount of stress that she experienced by writing: "The typical learning experience in the Emaze project was fun but stressful at the same time. Students really enjoyed taking pictures and having fun with the camera. It really got stressful at the end when we had to write the six paragraphs for the chosen photographs. Students were very busy trying to finish everything. They had to choose their six photos to write their paragraphs and it was getting hard because the paragraphs had to be submitted by the end of the week."

Because some students perceived that the time needed to complete the amount of work in the project was greater than the time allotted, some students expressed that they felt anxiety. A mid-level student lamented, "I am stressed and over-worked. I stayed up last night until 12 trying to finish my mass of homework and now I have to focus on this project all day. To[o] much work, not enough time." Furthermore, because some students felt the amount of work at times was too much, they were looking forward to the completion of the project. A low-achieving student commented, "I would feel stressed that I have to do all this work. I would look fo[r]ward to finishing all this."

Uniqueness of High- and Low-Achieving Groups

Low-Achieving Groups: Struggling with the Content

Even though students in all of the groups found the amount of work stressful, only low-achieving students commented about the difficulty they had with learning the technology required for the project. This difficulty may have been compounded due to the limited time available for the project. Even though these students struggled to learn how to use the digital camera, computer, and CSCL tools, they persisted in their efforts to master them. Typical of this group, one low-achieving student explained, "The girl . . . is getting frustrated because she is under so much pressure. She is beginning to get comfortable with the computer and the camera. She is determined to finish her research." Other low-achieving students commented that they met this challenge putting forth their best effort. One low-achieving student wrote: "There were many things I didn't get about technology and had hard times with certain things so I had to try my best."

High-Achieving Students: Learning at Their Own Pace

Some high-achieving students perceived that the project enabled them to learn at their own pace, and they reported being able to extend the learning activities throughout the day. One student described that the project made differentiation possible when he expressed, "The biggest difference is that in the typical learning experience the class moves together, but in the emaze solution experience we were able to move at our own pace."

For the high-achieving students, many of them were engaged in the project both inside and outside the designated class time. For instance, one student wrote: "I was always thinking about how I could get a picture from the different things going on around school. I feel like by doing that, that I was a true photographer and felt like my pictures came out really nice. I was always coming up with new ideas and shots."

These high-achieving students indicated that the CSCL project enabled the type of accelerated pacing that they valued.

Unique Experiences and Gender

Unique Experiences: Girls

In addition to the differences between achievement groups, there were differences between the genders as well. Only girls mentioned the novel experience of using computer technology to the extent provided by the CSCL project. Even though boys may not have used computer technology as intensely in class before, no boy commented on that. One girl described the novelty this way: "During this project I did more things on the computer than I had before. During this project I typed many things on the computer at school than I did before. Usually I would just go on the computer sometimes during school, but for this project I used the computer almost every day. The picture shows me writing the narrative for the emaze solutions project. During this project my classroom experience involved computers more than usual."

Other girls mentioned that they had never used a computer previous to this project. "Through the emaze project we all learned how to work computers, and how to work digital cameras. Some of us in the project never really used a computer before." Even though there were many girls who expressed how working on the computer was new to them, many other girls referred to using computers on previous assignments. For example, one girl commented, "Finally, the use of technology remains an ingrained part of our education since our school is one that focuses on science and technology. Many assignments are now done solely on the computer, such as research and essays."

Unique Experiences: Boys

Despite the range of experiences that girls reported about their level of previous computer usage, no boys commented on the novelty of using the computer during the project. Boys did mention the computer in their communications about the project but not as either more or less than in past experiences. There were no other themes unique to the boys in this project.

Implications of the Study

The findings of the CSCL study are consistent with research from the National Dropout Center that has identified alienation, apathy, frustration, and didactic lecture and note taking as continuing problems that influence student disengagement. Findings from this study also suggest that using CSCL projects to connect students to communities of practitioners and engage students in problem solving and knowledge building may be one way for educators and policymakers to deal with the problems of disengagement and dropout.

CSCL helps create new connections among students and online mentors that promote a sense of belonging. Because students often find schoolwork meaningless and disengage from learning, CSCL projects use online tools to enable students to create authentic products (e.g., essays, photographs, media presentations, and blogs) and situate generalized concepts into contexts both relevant and specific to students, all with the support and guidance of recognized experts at their fingertips. The findings suggest if students are helped in contextualizing content, students may begin to see the relevance of the material they are learning. One ancillary benefit to creating meaningful content is that students may change the quality of effort expended, transforming half-hearted attempts at participation into full-fledged endeavors to showcase their best work. This change may increase the number of students reaching mastery of subjects rather than merely achieving competency as students persist and extend their learning efforts.

CSCL environments are one way to differentiate the pacing for students in a group learning situation. By providing online, real-time, and asynchronous access to peer support, mentor assistance, exemplars, media examples, and websites, educators can help students either accelerate or remediate through content. Before CSCL projects can be employed in any large-scale effort, however, current online resources need further development for all content areas, topics, and state standards. Furthermore, current technologies are not adequate for supporting student learning. Some technologies are still too cumbersome or unreliable to adequately support all students or a large number of students. Some students still perceive the technology as frustrating and stressful.

Essential structural components of this project that secondary schools could utilize within their institutions include creating online, collaborative, knowledge-building environments with practitioners. Within this context, students would access new semiotic domains, social learning contexts, and online mentoring support from professional writers, photographers, scientists, artists, and others so that students may develop new affiliations with specialists and become prepared for future learning and career advancement. Through this access to appropriate domains, professional cultures, and contexts, students could be given the opportunity to learn how to speak, produce, problem solve, write, and build knowledge, based on specific semiotic domains. To implement these CSCL projects, classrooms need access to multimedia computers, broadband

Internet, and web portals with collaborative tools such as blogging and email. In these contexts, the application of generalized knowledge could be made specific and more relevant to students. As the researcher and author James Paul Gee suggests, by engaging in active learning of semiotic domains, students should be better prepared for learning in the future.

To replicate this project in secondary schools, participants need prior experience with knowledge-building activities in which they understand they are not merely consumers of knowledge but producers of it within the online environment.

Additionally, students need some prerequisite skills to interact in the online environment from basic computer and Internet search skills to conceptual knowledge of posting to online threads in asynchronous communication.

This knowledge-building environment needs to be fostered within the classroom culture in order to sustain student engagement. Because the support from media artifacts such as video, photographs, blogs, and hyperlinks are co-constructed in the online environment by the students themselves, participatory classroom cultures are needed to encourage and recognize student involvement. Classes of students in which knowledge is primarily transmitted through didactic lectures from teachers may find the participatory and constructive online environment unfamiliar. For CSCL projects to promote student engagement, a classroom culture that supports student inquiry is necessary.

CHAPTER 5

WHAT PARENTS WANT FROM THEIR CHILDREN'S SCHOOLS

WITH A TINGE OF FATHERLY ANXIETY, I remember bringing my six-year-old son, with his neatly combed blond hair and his nine-part cherub, one-part poltergeist personality, to the opening day of his school to meet his teacher. I introduced my son to the teacher, a petite woman from head to toe, generously proportioned around the middle. With the teacher standing before me, my son stared down at his feet shyly, partly leaning on me. This very happy, grandmotherly woman reached out her arms and said, "David come here." She embraced him in a hug that caused him to disappear in her welcoming arms, and continued, "David, we are going to have a great year together!" When I finally saw him emerge again from beneath the folds in her dress, I saw this sheepish grin on his face and my anxiety melted. The warmth and care I saw that day continued all year. That grandmotherly teacher loved my son, and she had my complete trust.

As parents, we may not all expect our child's teacher to welcome them with such enthusiasm, nor would most of our teenage children want that type of reception from their teacher; but underneath, we hope that the teacher will love our children at least a fraction of how much we love them. We put a tremendous amount of trust in the teachers of our children; and, for the most part, I have found teachers to be compassionate, caring, and ardent defenders of our kids. As an example of one of the many fine teachers I have met in the district in which I work, Mrs. Bristol coordinates the teen pregnancy program and watches over her teenage girls, teaches them, and cares for their babies like a mother lion. She ferociously protects her kids, and I've seen her more than one time take on a district administrator who was slow to act on a needed request for her kids. I can say, without a doubt, that she loves those kids like her own. As parents, we are relieved to know there are many Mrs. Bristols in the world who teach our children. In fact, in poll after poll, such as the annual Education Gallup Poll, when parents are asked about the quality of education in their own child's school and their own child's teacher, most parents give the local school and their child's teacher high marks (As and Bs).

In addition to a caring, compassionate teacher, parents of middle and high school students repeatedly make a similar request for what they want out of their children's education. At back-to-school nights, during parent evening, in classrooms, through phone calls, and even at coffeehouses, parents tell me they want teachers to inspire their children to reach their potential. One early morning, when I was talking to a mother of a middle school student and asked her what she saw as the purpose of school, she said, "To help her son aspire to become something more." Some parents have said it slightly differently, but many want the same thing for their children. Some say "they want the school to prepare their children to get good jobs or go to great universities." One feisty mother, in a phone call, told me she had one son who would go to the university ("he was always a good student"), but she worried about her other son who "did not have an academic bent. He did not know what he was going to do after high school" but "the school [and she meant me also] needed to do something for boys like hers to help them prepare to enter the job world." Recently, at the California League of Middle Schools' Awards Banquet for Distinguished

Middle School Teachers in our district, a letter from President Bush was read to those attending. His message connected with the parents and inspired the educators among us when he said good teachers "kindle the American Dream in our children."

James Truslow Adams in the 1930s first introduced the elusive concept of the American Dream in his book *The Epic of America* when he wrote that the American Dream is "that dream of a land in which life should be better and richer and fuller for everyone, with opportunity for each according to ability or achievement. It is not a dream of motor cars and high wages merely, but a dream of social order in which each man and each woman shall be able to attain to the fullest stature of which they are innately capable, and be recognized by others for what they are, regardless of the fortuitous circumstances of birth or position."

The aforementioned mother who had called me about her two sons wanted this American Dream for each of them, with their different abilities and achievement levels, but her hope sprang from the same fierce love for her two children. She wanted them, as James Truslow wrote, to "be able to attain to the fullest stature of which they were innately capable" of doing.

In addition to many parents agreeing on the purpose of education, many parents often agree about how their children should be educated. I had an opportunity to have some parents who were also school PTA presidents share their thoughts about education. Interestingly, there are some parallels between the themes from the students in the earlier chapters and what these parents wanted for their children. For example, the PTA parents also mentioned that personal one-on-one assistance was important, especially when their children were struggling to learn. Some parents just wanted to be notified if their child were not succeeding so that they could do something about it: "I would like to know if there is any way that the teachers can communicate to a parent of a student who is struggling before it is too late." Another parent, commenting on the importance of individual teacher-to-student assistance, wrote: "I would like teachers to set aside time for one-on-one time with each student on a regular basis. I believe that is the best way to understand their students and for the student to become comfortable with the teacher.

The more comfortable the students are with the teacher, the more willing they will be to express themselves."

Parents also mentioned they feel that the channels of communication that schools use are not sufficient to keep them informed: "The online grades are very helpful, but are not updated as often as needed. By the time the end of the first trimester came, the grades that were posted online were not the grades that came home on the report card."

In addition to the importance of one-on-one personal assistance, parents, like their sons and daughters, wanted the curriculum to be relevant. For example, one parent remarked, "I would like to see high school teachers use materials, information, and stories that my son can relate to. By making it personal, he would take a greater interest in listening to the teacher and thus actually hear what he is supposed to be listening to."

Another parent wrote: "I think it is so important to make learning relevant to students. This student engagement piece is critical to whether students tune into the learning or tune it out."

Another parallel between parents and students was the importance of an interactive curriculum in which students are actively involved in learning. One parent noted, "The interactivity of the curriculum is a key component." A second parent contended, "I would love to see projects done in various mediums other than essays; projects like the History Day, the USO show, and Junior Exhibition make learning more interesting, and students get to show off some talents that rarely get to be seen in the classroom anymore."

Another parent added, "I would love to see more teachers use an interactive curriculum that involves role-playing, music, art and lots of discovery learning."

Finally, parents often mentioned that student disinterest was a concern to them. For example, one parent wrote: "There is a general lack of understanding on the teachers' part that students get very bored. Bring it to a level that interests them. Understand that they are there to learn and it is a big disappointment to waste their time with a boring same ol' same ol' teaching style day after day."

Another parent explained, "I think when my children are given assignments that allow them to show some creativity in their work this engages them. Repetitious work tends to numb them and [they] rush to complete it rather than understand it."

I think, after reading the parent comments and the aforementioned student quotes, one might say, as the President of Sacred Heart, Dr. Cernera, articulated to an audience of university students and faculty, "that school is not always fun, it is hard work." This sentiment was echoed by author Thomas L. Friedman, who lamented that the educational work ethic of many students has degraded partially due to coddling parents. Friedman further illustrated his point when he shared a conversation he had with an accomplished student from Yale in which the distinguished graduate criticized other students who "want to do stuff that is fun. But there is no fun in algebra or memorizing the multiplication tables. But [those fundamentals] eventually become freshmen chemistry. And that's boring too . . . So it's not until you get to your senior level of advanced classes that you can start to have fun."

Based on my own experience and research, this assumption misses the underlying issue because most of the students and parents whom I interviewed are not expecting fun in class, nor do the parents with whom I have spoken want classes to be easy. In contrast, parents want a rigorous curriculum, as this parent mentioned: "I would like to see that kids that are ready for more of a challenge are provided an opportunity or forum to expand their education. Can there be competitions (either group or individual) that challenge all of a grade level?"

Parents ask us in education to provide instruction that is relevant, interactive, and meaningful in order to assist their children to reach their potential. Parents want their children to be challenged in school, and even many students want to work hard when they see the relevance of the studies. For example, even though some students in my research mentioned giving minimal effort in school when they found the work irrelevant, in the Emaze project these same students were willing to persist during difficulty, work long hours into the night, and work on the weekends in order to complete essays for the project.

A Tale of Two Classrooms

Students who have expectations of going on to the university or youths who come from families and communities with strong academic support in a particular content area may come into classes knowing the value of a particular subject and having sufficient background knowledge (e.g., a physician's child may have some background knowledge of anatomy and physiology) to make connections on their own between generalized concepts and particular examples. However, many of our kids need assistance from the teacher, practitioners, or other more capable peers to help them build background knowledge, create connections from new concepts to their existing knowledge, and construct meaning from new information.

I remember reading E.D. Hirsch's book *Cultural Literacy: What Every American Needs to Know*, in which he argued that it is important that all students know certain fundamental facts, words, scientific concepts, people, and places. I was a first-year, idealistic teacher at a wealthy private school and found his argument compelling enough to require my sixth graders to memorize and define 50 words a week from the list of important words found in the back of his book. At the beginning of the school year, I started with his *A* words and moved alphabetically through his list. At the beginning of each week, I assigned the list to the students, and I received positive responses from parents about this assignment even though some students disliked it. Despite the grumbling, students did the work; and if one didn't turn in the assignment, all I needed to do was call the parent and the homework appeared the next day.

The following year, still a very inexperienced teacher, I taught sixth grade at the poorest public school in the Lake Elsinore Unified School District. I had a student whose mother was a prostitute, a boy whose father had been arrested for selling speed, and another boy whose father and two uncles were in prison for theft. There were also parents who had to work two jobs to support their families. Many of these parents worked long hours. The reception I received was quite different when I again assigned the list of words.

The first week I assigned the words, most students failed to turn in the assignment the following week. To punish the students, I gave them detention, took away part of their recess, and even called parents—all to no avail. As I entered the scores into the grade book one day after school, the school's custodian came in to fix something in the room; hoping to get a sympathetic ear, I struck up a conversation, complaining that "these darn kids were lazy" and were not turning in their assignments. The janitor, John, in a gruff voice told me that he "didn't really see the importance of most of the subjects we taught, such as history and science." He did see the purpose of reading and some math skills, but "the rest of it was a waste of time for most of these kids." Not getting the response I wanted, I resumed entering grades in my book.

This did not deter me from continuing to assign the words from the list alphabetically and calling parent after parent when students failed to turn in the work (mostly to no avail). One day, during another phone call to Mrs. Allen, whom I had not seen at back-to-school night or any of the other opening school events, she gave a long sigh on the phone. She told me, "I can't get him to do his homework either. My husband isn't around, and I work late most nights, and my son is in bed before I get home." She then asked me, "Why are you assigning all these words [Solution, Algae, Volume, Surface Tension]? What's this got to do with anything they'll need to know to get a job? My son isn't the college type."

To be honest, I don't remember what I said; but I do remember thinking that I wasn't at Sacred Heart School anymore. The parents and students just didn't get it. I reluctantly admitted to myself that I needed to do something different. What I didn't know was that I was the one who didn't get it. These were hardworking blue-collar parents who had to work long hours to support their families, and some, like Mrs. Allen, who didn't know exactly why her child needed to learn this, put their trust in me, and I was breeching that trust by failing to engage their children. Even though, at the time, I took Mrs. Allen's question as a sign that she was not supporting me, she gave me a clue that day ("Why are you assigning…?"). I wasn't doing a good job of making the connection for the students between what they were learning and the relevance it played in their lives and their future.

However, being a bit daft, again this did not deter me; I kept on assigning the words. But not long after that, on a hot day in September when the lake (only a mile from the school) had an algae bloom and the smell of dead fish wafted towards our classroom, one of the kids asked why the lake always stunk and why the fish kept dying. The thought struck me that this might be the basis of a lesson unit, and I quickly jotted down some notes. That evening I spent until late in the night planning my "Lake Unit," in which we would incorporate the vocabulary from our science and some of Hirsh's list of words.

The next day, I had students generate questions they had about the stinky lake with the blue green algae painted on the lake's bank. From those questions, we created a list that we would work to answer through the course of the unit. (I also arranged for a field trip to the lake to gather water samples for measuring algae, nitrogen, and phosphorous levels.) I adjusted my infamous list to include words from our unit that would be due after we covered the knowledge and concepts as part of the Lake Unit. Additionally, students emailed the water district's biologist with a list of interview questions, and students incorporated his answers and the vocabulary words into a Hyperstudio presentation with digital photographs of our samples and observations from the lake. The students received some local newspaper attention about their findings, and even the Public Relations Officer representing the local water district that partially controlled the lake's water supply began calling us and talking with our students. (You can imagine, we were a PR nightmare for the water district, which was trying to encourage vacationers to ski and fish on the lake; the "stinky" lake quotes from the kids weren't generating the type of press they wanted. However, they were very kind to our kids, and they kept their concerns to themselves, eagerly giving our students information about the lake.) Our class did experiments based on the questions students generated while other students began doing their own experiments using the data gathered about the lake. We incorporated some of our math concepts and formulas by doing algorithmic calculations of the results data.

After more than one month on the unit, students were ready to share their findings with the community and parents. As we were planning our presentation, the custodian, John, popped into the hall where we were feebly trying to create a makeshift stage for the presentation and asked if we needed any help. We were eager to accept his assistance, and his expertise became apparent as he built us a stage complete with props over the next week leading up to the presentation. After he finished the stage and the students finished their research, the students presented their findings to a packed audience of parents and community members. Mrs. Allen sat beaming in the audience that night as her son Danny, along with others, explained their findings. My kids were so proud of how hard they had worked and what they had accomplished. However, I think their parents were more proud.

Even though some students participated at lower levels than others and other students didn't think the activity was fun, student engagement was high, student participation increased, and the percentage of students completing the definitions of the infamous list of words rose dramatically. That year, I even saw an increase in standardized scores in the area of math (science wasn't tested by the state at that time). As an ancillary benefit to the project, I became good friends with John the custodian, who, on a series of Saturdays on his own time, built me a life-size ancient Greek temple for our unit on Greece. Periodically, he checked on my kids to see how they were doing, and they responded to his interest by sharing what they were learning. Later, he even worked with the students on weekends and after school to create a koi pond complete with a solar-powered waterfall and rimmed with flagstone. I don't know if he ever changed his mind about whether he thought science and history were important; however, I do know that his engagement and interest in my students' learning was important to them. His interest and the community and parent support for the Lake Presentation all helped to create value for the learning we were doing and further engaged the students.

I still believe E.D. Hirsch makes a compelling argument for cultural literacy, but when I assigned lists of words to students without the proper background information, relevance, or visual supports, I failed my students. Simply dismissing students as "lazy" because I assumed that they were expecting fun instead of hard work missed the point. Not until I helped to create meaning for the students from questions they asked and related it to their personal experiences were students able to make meaning from the vocabulary and science I was assigning.

When a student or a parent asks for an interesting, meaningful curriculum, we as educators should not trivialize the request as a euphemism for fun. Instead, their request should be honored as a reminder to us of what it means to bring excellence to education, for if we have an interactive, effective curriculum, we will help to create the conditions that will engage students, and we might find that we are able to resolve the problem of student dropout and disengagement.

CHAPTER 6

WHAT SCHOOLS CAN LEARN FROM STARBUCKS, SCRAPBOOKING, AND DEEP-SEA FISHING

WHAT MAKES THE EDUCATION that we enthusiastically acquired by getting a cup of coffee at Starbucks, constructing a scrapbook through Creative Memories, or sportfishing on the *Qualifier 105* so similar? What can our 21st-century schools learn from these effective learning experiences? I didn't realize the quality of education that Starbucks provided (work with me here) until I saw the transformation of my wife from an occasional, once-a-year coffee drinker to a full-fledged Mocha Mystic in just a few short visits to Starbucks. I persuaded her to go to Starbucks after convincing her there was more to coffee than the black bitter drink she had during late nights in college. We walked into one of their many well-lit, aromatic, bakery-filled stores. My wife gazed at the colorful green-and-red menus, chocolate-packaged coffee roasts, photographs of customers on the wall, and tasty pictures of Cinnamon Dolce Lattes reading: "The beverage of beautiful buttery bliss is back." Alliteration was never so delightfully delicious.

Three women met around slices of coffee cake conversing in soft but enthusiastic tones. A couple waited around the espresso machine that spurted out heat and steam as a small white cloud formed from the condensing vapor above the black bar. My wife asked me what might be good and, knowing that she loved chocolate, I told her that a whipped cream-topped mocha would be a good starter. We walked to the counter and the woman standing behind the register greeted us with a warm welcome. After I asked for my tall coffee, my wife stumbled out her request for a medium mocha. The woman politely asked for her name and then spoke to the barista: "Eileen needs a Grande Mocha with whip." After getting our drinks, my wife sipped her beverage and with a touch of whipped cream on her lips raised both eyebrows and said that "it was quite good." When she saw my drink, she did seem a bit perplexed when my tall drink was smaller than her medium. "Shouldn't asking for a tall coffee get you a large drink rather than requesting a tall coffee when you really want a small drink?"

I could tell that my wife was warming to this coffee shop experience because about a month later when we were driving "about," she asked if I wanted to get some coffee. We walked up to the counter and this time she asked for "a grande, decaf, low-fat, white mocha with whip." She looked at me to see my mouth drop just a little. Wow! What a difference a month makes. Starbucks had (coincidentally or purposefully) operationalized the components of social constructivism to make an engaging and tasty learning environment.

According to social constructivists, learners construct knowledge within the context of social interactions. Unlike behavioralists, such as Skinner, who theorize that behavior is only strengthened or weakened by consequences of punishments or rewards (however, a white mocha sure makes a powerful reward), social constructivists theorize learners build their own understanding of the world collaboratively through a process of "meaning making." My wife was safely able to explore the coffee shop and test different drinks all within the context of a social interaction with the barista, friends, and me. By interacting within this small community, she was able to hear (e.g., grande), see (e.g., menus), and use (e.g., ordering) the language she perceived as meaningful (e.g., to getting her mocha) and begin to internalize the communications (e.g., she was able to order on her own). Throughout this learning process, she communicated interpersonally with more skilled Starbuck members (e.g., baristas) and community members who served to support the learning. The value of this place and its products was further reinforced by her friends, the media, and even the small group of ladies with whom my wife identified within an atmosphere of stimulating conversation, smooth drinks, and tasty goodies. The great researcher Lev Vygotsky would be watching proudly and sipping a White Russian coffee if he was alive to see such an obvious manifestation of his social constructivist theory.

Furthermore, I would note one other modern, important component to this successful learning environment that Starbucks has incorporated, as so many other successful retail, service and restaurant corporations of the 21st century have, into their shop cultures: They have combined an environment of social inclusion with personalization. Starbucks has enabled people within a community context to shape their experience (e.g., creating their own drinks, tacking photographs of themselves on the community board) as customers by allowing them to express their unique interests, needs, and characteristics. People have an opportunity to voice their individuality. Even though this social, yet personal experience is done much better by Starbucks than many others, this occurrence is common in the 21st century not only in commercial services but community and online experiences—such as party quests from the online game Maple Story—as well. The Net Generation youths have been nurtured in this type of environment where they have come to value not only social learning opportunities but personal ones within the community context.

Of course, the complexity of what we teach in our schools requires additional strategies that go beyond the learning of the language, symbols, signs, and culture of ordering a drink in a coffee shop (although, less so than we might think). However, let us consider the highly effective education that adults and youths receive outside of school without ever hearing a lecture, taking notes, or answering questions from the end of a chapter. Whether it is scrapbooking or sportfishing on the *Qualifier 105*, beginners quickly become adept by embedding the skills, concepts, and knowledge into the activity, context, and culture in which it occurs. My wife has never answered questions in the back of the book to learn how to operate her punchpress, use the trimmer, or scallop the edge of a matte for scrapbooking and yet she, her friends, and millions of others have learned to use the technologies, apply new designs, and create beautiful page layouts. Nor have I crammed all night to memorize and identify dozens of ocean fish (e.g., bluefin, dorado, calico bass) or to set the drag to land a 60-pound yellowfin tuna on a 40-pound test line or even how to tie a dropper loop to catch yellowtail off Benitos Island. (I do have to admit, much to my wife's dismay, that she has caught me examining the centerfold from a deep-sea fishing magazine of a 90-pound yellowtail beauty; she's even found me trolling the Internet for fishing reports.) However, this interest in reading about fishing only occurred after many engaging learning experiences on the *Qualifier 105*, *Vagabond*, and other deep-sea fishing boats that hooked my interest (okay I went for the easy pun).

All of this learning is embedded into the fishing or scrapbooking activity Just in Time. Just in Time support means information is provided to the learner at the moment the student needs the information to solve a problem or make a decision in order to perform the operation, skill, or tactic required for the next step in the process. As adults complete these tasks, such as setting the drag on a fishing reel, others are there to support, offer suggestions, and provide exemplars within this subculture of sport-fishing. A novice deep-sea fishing enthusiast (some of you may be surprised that such a person could exist) learns to catch the fastest, healthiest anchovy in the bait tank or to tie the right kind of knot. Oftentimes, in contrast to school where we teach content such as grammar weeks before students actually get to use the skills in writing, this Just in Time fishing education is not taught in a lecture weeks before the activity of fishing but rather only moments before the enthusiast ties the knot for the very first time.

Even learning to tie the knot itself is done within the context of fishing rather than in isolation as a series of discreet, independent activities as schools often do to teach the skills in the subjects of writing and science. The novice fisherman can clearly see the connection of learning to tie the knot as important to securing the hook to the line in order to catch the fish. However, some students don't always clearly see the connection of learning to select the correct usage of "me" or "I" on a worksheet to becoming a better writer. Research suggests students are more engaged in learning concepts and skills when learning is embedded into the activity that requires the skill or concept.

Additionally, the novice user in sportfishing is closely mentored by the community of more experienced fishermen and fisherwomen on the boat. For example, the deckhand models the knot and then gives the beginner a chance to try on his or her own with guided practice from the expert. After tying the knot, the novice gets immediate feedback from the deckhand, who examines the knot and will either reteach it or

My son learning to catch the healthiest and fastest anchovy in the bait tank!

give his or her approval. Later novices find out if they acquired the knowledge when they tie their own knot and, after hooking a fish, either bring the fish aboard or lose it due to the faulty knot. Of course, there is plenty of food, drink, engaging conversation, and lots of examples to help the beginner through this fundamental exercise.

This rich and authentic setting contrasts with the sterile environment of many secondary classrooms with the only examples of exemplar work lying hidden from novices behind the papers of more capable peers. Okay, enough about fishing, the point being that the learning theory of social constructivism provides a heuristic framework that explains how knowledge is acquired, a process by which students engage the community through discourse and thus build knowledge in authentic social situations. Additionally, if schools could better operationalize some of the elements of social constructivism, such as embedding learning within the context of the activities in a Just in Time approach, many students would be more engaged.

Another tenet of social constructivism can be observed by watching why many flock to scrapbooking parties. Even though my wife had fiddled around with some simple page layouts scrapbooking on her own, I began to see a creative flair after she attended a couple scrapbooking functions. My spouse's friend, Tami, invited my wife and daughter to attend a wild party of late-night scrapbooking. At our house we are usually in bed by 10:00 P.M. on a Saturday night and so this time I was the one dismayed to find my wife and daughter straggle in after midnight (intoxicated with elation from cutting, pasting, and organizing photographs). The next morning she and my daughter proudly shared their pages that they had worked hard to complete late into the night. We all went through the layouts of their scrapbook, page by page. They both discussed their scrapbook, comparing and contrasting what they had done with others from the party. Through the opportunity to customize their pages and layouts within the supportive context of sharing examples and ideas within this small community, my wife and daughter persisted in the highly engaging environment. This activity combines both the opportunity to connect with others while expressing and voicing their uniqueness by personalizing their own scrapbooks. My daughter and wife had not simply acquired knowledge from the other members, but through their interactions they contributed to the behaviors, ideas, values, and work of the community wherein they were invited to participate further in the form of other scrapbooking parties. The renowned researchers Lave and Wenger suggest in their seminal research on situated learning in social constructivism that learning occurs as the student and community are reconstituted through engagement and interaction as novice and experienced members contribute to the collective knowledge of the community.

In order to operationalize this into our schools, educators need to give our students opportunities to contribute their work, knowledge, and ideas to the community. Whether it is the high-tech online environment of MySpace or the low-tech environment of scrapbooking parties, the Net Generation has grown up contributing to the community by customizing their work in social contexts. Digital technology itself is not as important as the characteristics that digital technology is able to facilitate such as personalization, Just in Time learning, immediate feedback, social connections, authentic learning contexts, and knowledge contributions. When students are given opportunities to share their abilities, students are given further occasions to engage in meaningful activities that the community at large can affirm (e.g., as we all did as a family the next morning by going through the layouts of my wife's and daughter's photographs). By encouraging their undertakings, the content that was acquired and then resynthesized is given further value that in turn supports future efforts by other students in the community as they see the work, knowledge, and ideas being valued.

CHAPTER 7

SOLUTIONS TO THE PROBLEM OF STUDENT DROPOUT AND DISENGAGEMENT

THE SOLUTIONS TO THE problem of student dropout and disengagement can be mitigated by parents and educators working together and focusing on both making meaning of the learning for our youth and facilitating the acquisition of new skills and knowledge. Unfortunately, the importance of both of these latter two goals has often been hotly debated in a dichotomous argument. As one assistant principal told me, she "didn't want her teachers spending time developing background knowledge for students because there wasn't enough time in the year to do that." Or a central office administrator telling me "there isn't enough time to use technology." Or a teacher explaining that "having students write, edit and rewrite an essay was too time consuming," and that instead she had her students "do short timed writing exercises in class because it better prepared her students for the state test." Another teacher told me that "even though writing for an authentic audience or presenting findings might be motivating, it wasn't important for learning." This may have been a backlash against the educational philosophy that focused on the "new math," "whole language," "self-esteem building" period of the nineties in which "getting the correct answer wasn't necessary as long as students knew the process." The same period allowed students to use a "naming word" instead of expecting them to know what a noun was or permitted students to calculate the wrong answer in math as long as they knew the process. This commonly accepted educational notion put our students further behind in the international community according to such indicators as the TIMMS report, which compares countries' proficiency levels in math and science.

Accepting student meaning making without expecting our students to acquire the language and processes commonly used in the culture and community severely handicaps our students' ability to compete in the new globalization of the workforce. However, as educators, if we rush through concepts without enabling students to connect new knowledge to previous understanding, building background knowledge, or providing visuals and experiences, we are deluding ourselves into thinking that we are teaching our children to learn. The shock from the research of a rising dropout rate of 32% and the research suggesting that 66% of students disengage during instruction should jar us from our status quo practices of "doing our jobs grinding through the book and state standards" (an actual quote from my child's teacher at back-to-school night) even if the students aren't engaged.

In order to equip students of the Net Generation with the ability to build skills and make meaning, we need to create relevant, personal, community-connected, and rigorous learning environments and curriculum. By utilizing new digital technologies such as email and classroom websites now available in the classroom to educators and leveraging the rising culture of connection and collaboration, our educational system can open the gates that closed the campus to the community, can connect parents and educators cut off from contact by the nonexistent communication technologies in classrooms (e.g., most classrooms did not even have phones until the late nineties), and transform the anachronistic, isolationalist, cultural practices of many schools that blocked collaboration efforts. However, digital educational technologies cannot in and of themselves create the necessary change but rather they merely create the conditions for this change. Rather it is the educators, with the help of parents, who can transform schools into modern, dynamic learning environments. Just because it is possible for an administrator at a school to drop a quick email to a parent about their child, that capability to communicate doesn't mean that it will happen. We need the ability and the will to make it happen.

Relevant Learning

As I do "walk bouts" in countless classrooms, I often see teachers trying to make learning relevant to students by telling them that "one day you will need this [skill, knowledge, algorithm] in college or your career." The research study that I did suggests that with the exception of the high-achieving, "A" student who knows they are going to college (and not even always with this group), this college reference does not make learning relevant or meaningful to students. In the study, only 16% of the students found this a compelling reason to remain engaged in learning. The other 84% of learners need other supports to make learning relevant to them.

What Can Schools and Districts Do?

Through application of information, Just in Time learning, producing and consuming information, and creativity, many youths are able to find the relevance of learning new knowledge and skills. Schools and districts can provide robust and rich curriculum to schools that emphasizes new skills, knowledge, and the implementation of applied concepts. *The Kansas City Star* in November of 2006 reported how eight metro-area school districts adopted Project Lead the Way, a high school and middle school pre-engineering curriculum that not only teaches physical science, Boolean algebra, and calculus but provides meaningful activities in which students learn how to apply the knowledge and concepts into applications. Students create models of objects with 3-D industry specific imaging software, design circuits, test the load and force capacity of their self-designed building structures, and program robots. Knowledge and concepts are not taught in the abstract but contextualized into specific situations. As cited in the article, one coordinator of the program said, "It comes to life. It's the 'Now what?' part of it."

Students not only learn to contextualize the knowledge but learn how to transfer that understanding to new situations. As part of the culminating project, students have an opportunity to apply much of what they learned. Take Sarah, for example, the high school girl in Saratoga who despised having to start her car and wait in the freezing temperatures until the heater warmed up the vehicle. Because of this problem, she invented a cell phone-activated car starter in the final class of the Project Lead the Way program. With a three-digit call to the vehicle, the car starts up and now when she enters her vehicle she is greeted with the warmth of the heater even as ice and snow freezes everything outside the car. As part of her invention, she presented a PowerPoint of the relays, wiring, and circuits it took to design her creation. Additionally, she has had her invention patented for the new global market waiting for her unique application of science, math, ingenuity, and creativity. The curriculum of Project Lead the Way is not only engaging but also preparatory for students entering the demands of the 21st-century global workforce. Relevance is not an ancillary consideration but fundamental to learning and provides a powerful solution to the problem of student disengagement.

What Can Teachers Do?

Teachers can help students see the relevance of new knowledge and content by having students answer essential questions, solve a problem, or make a decision. Essential questions are the big ideas in which a unit of study can be organized. The educational author and reformer Grant Wiggins suggests that we can better engage our students by organizing "courses not around 'answers' but around questions and problems to which 'content' represent answers." Examples of these questions might be: Is the American Dream still important today? How has the global economy affected the American workforce?

Questions like these require students to acquire basic knowledge and facts in order to analyze and synthesize a response to the essential underlying issue. In this model, teachers create a purpose and an application for the information presented in a unit of study by providing a compelling reason to learn. Asking students to memorize a definition of the American Dream because it will be important to know in college is not as applicable to knowing the definition in order to critically examine the importance of that American Dream today. Students need to know the facts and basic understanding of the content so that later they can apply that information into an individual response of the essential question. The essential question provides the "So what?" to the information.

I have found a highly engaging model for embedding these essential questions into a new type of format—an email simulation—that we have found in our research studies raises student achievement and engages students. In an email simulation, students are transported back into time or into a literature book and are able to communicate with historical figures or fictional characters. Students resolve a conflict and answer essential questions using email to communicate with historical figures like Thomas Jefferson or Ramses II. In literature, students get to interact with characters like Dr. Jekyll and Mr. Hyde in order to explore a book's theme. The central core of the electronic exercise is to have students make a decision by gaining knowledge through communication, gathering resources, analyzing information, and then developing a product. We have used community specialists, university professors, and even district personnel to give life to the characters in history and literature. Special email accounts are created in which these community members take on the personae of the character. There are distinctive communication tasks these characters complete with the students that lead students through the process of answering essential questions and, ultimately, to making decisions about the characters. Email becomes the tool to foster channels of communication with the community, extend the learning opportunities for students, apply knowledge, and engage students.

Examples of specific simulations include ones in which students travel back in time to Civil War-era America in order to resolve the conflict and unite a future community. The students must answer the question: Did the South have the right to secede from the union? Students communicate with Jefferson Davis, President Lincoln, Robert E. Lee, and an abolitionist through email. Students must eventually advise President Lincoln and Jefferson Davis on whether the South had the right to withdraw from the Union.

In another simulation, sixth grade students are asked by the god Osiris to judge the lives of Cleopatra and Ramses II. Are Cleopatra and Ramses II worthy to go into the afterlife? Students weigh and measure these Pharaohs' lives to determine if their accomplishments outweighed the human rights abuses they inflicted on their people. The students correspond with Cleopatra, Ramses II, Osiris, and slaves from that time. Cleopatra and Ramses II email a summary of their accomplishments as well as websites, graphics, etc., to the student to persuade him or her of their greatness. The slave emails the student a summary of the mistreatment that the ancient Egyptians suffered at the hands of these two rulers. The students then report to Osiris what they learned as well as their commentary on the situation. Ultimately, students determine whether Cleopatra and Ramses will be passing through to the afterlife after measuring the merits of their accomplishments against the weight of their human rights atrocities. These email simulations promote relevance, engagement, and achievement by structuring the learning activities around essential questions.

What Can Parents Do?

In April of 2006, I was invited by the publisher of Santa Monica Press to come to the L.A. Times Festival of Books at UCLA. I had heard that Julie Andrews and Billy Crystal were going to be there, so I invited the rest of my family to attend with me. The memory of the long drive, bickering children, and the frustration from a couple of wrong turns dissipated as soon as we pulled up to the beautiful UCLA campus, heralded by a refreshing breeze and a sunny Southern California day. My two kids were mildly interested in the booths as we walked between the aisles, but their interest peaked when they got to talk with Andrea Lankford, the author of *Haunted Hikes,* and hear about spine-tingling tales and trails from North America's National Parks. However, the highlight of the trip was the experience of walking on the UCLA campus. Both kids pointed to buildings and places on campus asking my wife and me about the classes, the dorms, the length of time students attended, types of classes, and dozens of other questions. I'm a University of California at Irvine graduate, so you can imagine my disappointment by their new-found interest in going to UCLA. However, I was secretly pleased by the serendipitous fortune of having my two children talking about going to college, even if it was at the rival UCLA. To add to the experience our day ended not only with bags of books from the fair but with a trip to the UCLA bookstore and two Bruin T-shirts for both the kids. (I wonder if I bought them a shirt with the UCI Anteater if they might reconsider their college selection!) One year later, both my kids still like wearing their shirts and even continue to express an interest in attending UCLA.

After just a day at the university, my son and daughter could imagine themselves attending classes there and visualize themselves walking around on the campus. The experience had done something that my numerous talks with them for their future had been unable to do. With a stroll on the campus and a blitzkrieg of questions, they had created a meaningful, clear picture of their future. As parents, one of the most powerful ways we can make learning relevant is to provide experiences for our kids that connect background knowledge and present-day educational opportunities to future academic and career possibilities. These experiences are not necessarily limited to field trips to universities but can also include opportunities to intern or visit a family member's place of employment. For as students walk, talk, and experience glimpses of a possible future, our children begin to see the nexus between their present life and who they might become.

Personal Learning

What Can Administrators and Teachers Do?

Along with the principal, I was at a high school doing "walk bouts," which involve visiting classrooms to assess how students are learning. For about the third or fourth time that day we walked into the classroom to see the teacher sitting down as students worked independently answering questions from a worksheet or from a textbook. Most students did seem to be working in this fairly disciplined class and the teacher was comfortable with the principal and me walking around asking the kids questions.

I ambled over to several students to see what they were learning. In this class, students were doing a fractions worksheet; one student was struggling to write something on the paper, a couple of students had answered incorrectly despite showing the steps they had taken to solve the problems, and another student told me that it was pretty easy and was finishing up his last couple problems. I determined that the teacher had conducted an intensive lecture prior to the worksheet and now it was the students' turn to practice what they had learned. We stayed long enough to hear the teacher say that if they didn't finish the assignment it was due for homework the next day. I assumed the teacher would correct the assignment after they turned it in and in a couple of days the students would get feedback. Even though the teacher had done her job of instructing and providing a safe and well-managed classroom, many of the students still had not learned the content and needed additional aid. The feedback that would be coming in two days would not be adequate to help the students who needed the assistance at that moment. Students needed additional Just in Time support to their learning that they were not getting.

In contrast to this experience, I had the opportunity to continue my visits and see a math classroom that better met the needs of our Net Generation students. This time a group of at-risk students were working on a computer program called ALEKS. The program provided not only questions in pre-algebra and algebra but tutorials for students who moved at their own pace through the math class as well. When students missed a question, the program gave them feedback immediately. When students were stuck, the program offered support, with the steps needed to solve the problem, and then gave the students another question of the same type to determine if they had mastered it. I saw a dedicated teacher moving from student to student assisting youths when the computer instruction was not sufficient. I asked a couple of students what they thought of this format and all but one girl said that they "liked it better than the regular classes." (The one girl said she "missed being able to talk with friends.") When I inquired as to why they liked it better, I was told by several that they liked "moving at their own rate." After a few minutes, the teacher came up to me and enthusiastically showed me a real-time report of the progress students had made during that class period, which included not only the problems they answered correctly or incorrectly but aggregated the results to show which specific content standards students had mastered and those for which they needed further assistance. The teacher also told me that "they were very proud to be able to offer variable credit to students based on the students' progress during the course. Some students may progress at a slower rate and get pre-algebra credit for the class, but for those students who moved at a quicker pace, they would be able to get algebra credit for the class." Not only was the program customizing the learning environment, but the administrative and teaching team was also aiding in personalizing the students' education by responding to the individual needs and growth of the students.

Despite the contrasting experiences, the conclusion that I drew was not that every student should be taught in a computer lab with Computer Assisted Math Instruction (however, it does have its place). Rather this Net Generation more than any other expects a personalized educational setting that meets their needs, provides immediate feedback, and enables them to move at their own rate. These individualized aspects can be provided without technology, however the time and complexity of teaching a customized curriculum for 35 students all at one time is arguably difficult.

Some educators are implementing a technology solution that promotes a personalized atmosphere for students by using response pads sold by companies like Turning Point Technologies and Qwizdom. A response pad is a small device that looks like a television remote, which connects wirelessly to a teacher's console and which gives the teacher knowledge instantly about whether students understand a concept. As a teacher is instructing, she may ask the students a question to check for understanding. The students press a button to indicate the answer from a selection of multiple-choice answers. Instantly every student's answer is transmitted to the teacher, who can assess whether students understand the material. The teacher gets a list of the names of students who got it correct and those who got it incorrect. However, the real customization of the content comes as a result of that information. The teacher can determine that some of the students are ready for independent practice and assign them classwork, and for the students who still need help, teachers can work with those students in a small group setting or help them in a one-on-one context.

Of course, even without the aid of computers or response pads, while more difficult, good teachers across the country do assist students one-on-one and work with small groups of struggling students, as other more capable students practice independently. One of the barriers to this type of personalized instruction is often different perceptions about how independent students should be. Some educators say statements like: "They need to learn [without extra support]; they are in high school now." Or in middle schools, I often hear: "We need to prepare them for high school. So, they better learn it [no special treatment] now!" Unfortunately, with this attitude not only are many of our at-risk students not learning, but they are dropping out as well. Students who "don't get it" don't learn by being ignored or by being punished into acquiring knowledge but rather some need more customized supports than we are currently providing.

What Can Parents Do?

Using the textbook as my primary means of instruction, I was teaching my class of middle school students in Lake Elsinore about earthquakes. Even though the book did have a great photograph of the San Andreas Fault, the picture only warranted a momentary examination by my kids, who were otherwise uninterested. After school one day, I had a breakthrough on the subject. One parent told me that a local fault line ran through the Lake Elsinore area. The fault line traversed a place where his son rode his motorbike and had paintball fights with his friends. The boy hadn't told me about this in class (maybe because I hadn't bothered to ask), however, he became a local hero the next day as I had him share that he played on a fault line. The kids all wanted to know exactly where it was and others soon realized that they too had played near the fault. Students asked me if they could go on the Internet and find information about it. For the next couple of weeks, whenever I could, I tied my lesson and content into that local example. Student engagement rose substantially for this unit as a result of this parent's participation.

Even though I ended up using the parent's contribution in my classroom, these types of personal examples can be shared by parents with their own children. As parents, we can increase our child's interest in a subject if we can suggest connections between the content our children are learning at school and local examples, personal experiences, and family outings. Through these types of supports, we can promote intellectual connections between meaningful examples and new content knowledge that makes the learning personal for our sons and daughters.

World War II never became so personal to my daughter than when our family visited Check Point Charlie and its interactive museum in Berlin and she touched the Berlin Wall and heard the stories of those who had escaped from East Berlin. My daughter became interested in reading the diary of Anne Frank because of this experience. She read several other books that summer about the people and times of WWII and of those who were caught in the East after the war. Later she told me that her trip to Berlin promoted and sustained her interest in the unit on World War II at school. Visiting, seeing, and touching the Berlin Wall had sparked the interest in doing the more academic work of reading both nonfiction and historical fiction. Both were important to making her a better learner. The experience created the motivation and curiosity in which to contextualize the stories and information from the books she would read.

For another family outing, we went to Mission San Juan Capistrano while my son was learning about the missions at school. My son took digital photographs of where the Indians worked, artifacts from the museum, and (his favorite picture) a lizard sunning itself on a rock. As a result of the experience, that week when he was asked to write about the missions, he wrote one of his best pieces of expository writing. Learning about the missions had become personal to him because of his contact with them. As parents we can support and improve our children's chances for student engagement by creating opportunities for hands-on experiences and storytelling in our own homes.

To further support this notion that these types of personal experiences are important to learners, I had heard Dr. Kim from UCI speak about a study he had done comparing low, middle and high socioeconomic students. He found that students from high socioeconomic families showed larger gains on state exams after being home during the summer than the gains they achieved at school during the year. In comparison, students from middle and low socioeconomic families displayed much smaller gains or, in some cases, no gains at all during the summer. The results of the study did not answer why this was true but I suspect that it was related to the differences between the places students from higher socioeconomic families had visited, the dialogues they had shared, the books they had read, and the science camps and other summer educational experiences that affluent children had experienced as compared to other students. During the summer, students of higher socioeconomic backgrounds had greater opportunities to make the learning that schools test and assess meaningful through firsthand summer experiences.

To be able to extend these types of quality, outside-of-school experiences to all children, parents and educators need to create strong partnerships in order to focus resources, efforts, and skills in connecting the coursework inside of school to opportunities that parents can provide outside of school. As parents, we may not always know what our children are learning or which circumstances outside of school might best promote learning content standards inside of school. But with parents and educators working together, parents would know what and how they could support their child's education. Through these partnerships we would produce better educated students.

Connected Community

By creating partnerships and supporting student collaboration with scientists, artists, writers, and researchers, students could be given opportunities to connect with those who can promote a sense of belonging and inclusion within the larger community outside of school. For example, one nonprofit organization, ACME, has been highly successful at helping secondary school students become professional animators. The nonprofit provides an online mentoring service to classes of students where students are matched with professional animators from such studios as Warner Brothers and Disney who mentor them in online discussions and critique the students' work on the ACME website. Through online collaboration, students have opportunities to display their work and access knowledge, skills, and support from animation professionals. By participating in this network, students have the opportunity to benefit from the shared knowledge that ultimately promotes students' greater inclusion into a technologically advancing society.

Another online mentoring project, Project GLOBE, has been highly successful at increasing student achievement and engaging middle school students through an inquiry-based, computer-supported collaborative learning application that was designed to engage middle and high school students in problem solving with peers and scientists through GLOBE email, online threaded discussions, and online media objects. Students are able to compare and contrast their findings from different experiments conducted as part of the project with the findings of other classes of students, all the while being supported by scientists who mentor the kids throughout the experiments.

By providing students with opportunities to connect with these networks of skilled practitioners, students are given the chance to collaborate with professionals who further reinforce the value of what is being taught. Additionally, students get to assume an identity as a scientist, writer, animator, or other specialist because they are engaging in collaborative projects with practitioners who promote a sense of authenticity in the work. Through this exploration, the research suggests students begin to perceive an affinity with these groups that promotes a sense of belonging and improves student engagement.

Rigor

What is a rigorous education? Is it knowing one's basic math facts and reading to the level of comprehension? Is it knowing and using the language of a discipline? Is it learning algorithms or processes to find answers and solutions? Is it applying knowledge to a situation? Is it critical thinking and problem solving? Is it researching, synthesizing, and writing? Is it utilizing and producing with digital technologies? Rigor is all of these and settling for less in any aspect is accepting a form of mediocrity that numbs our children into "apathy" and sentences our educational system into obsolescence. Even if we have agreement on these requirements, how do we proceed forward in our schools and classrooms to deliver the full spectrum of rigorous education?

Curriculum needs to be restructured so that within every single unit of study, students move from basic skills and comprehension, to the ability to analyze and apply facts, and, finally, to the capacity to synthesize and evaluate. Within units of learning, students need to be both effective consumers of information (e.g., memorizing and comprehending) as well as producers of knowledge (e.g., writing, authoring, digital production). Some say that there isn't enough time to structure curriculum in this manner and would rather see us cover thousands of concepts cursorily than learning and synthesizing essential knowledge in depth. With this dichotomous argument one could argue quantity vs. quality. However, the reality of how most children learn does not enable students to scan and save information to their organic, dendritic hard drive as a computer does. Most students need to make meaning out of information and processes as well as apply it in order to remember it. Without this last step, the information becomes what researchers call inert knowledge (information that the learner doesn't know how to use or operationalize in the real world). With this understanding of how people learn, the old argument of breadth of knowledge vs. depth of knowledge is analogous to discussing how many angels can sit on the head of a pin. We need to take time in teaching to make certain that students are learning the content as opposed to ensuring that we in education are instructing all the content.

There are many ways to build a rich curriculum that promotes the full spectrum of student skills and mental processes (e.g., application, analysis, synthesis, evaluation). One way that has been highly effective for us at engaging students and raising student achievement is by embedding digital technologies into six phases of a unit of study. A unit of study groups related concepts and procedures (e.g., algorithms, scientific phases) over a period of time from one to four weeks. This contrasts with a series of loosely grouped, independent, chronological daily lessons with little or no tie to previous concepts. The six phases of the unit include the following:

1. Inquiry Phase—Engaging students in the initial question, problem, or decision through interrogative strategies, short discussion, presentation of real-world problems, virtual media objects, and/or experiential learning opportunities.
2. Information Phase—Direct multimedia instruction of the basic skills, concepts, algorithms, and processes of the unit with opportunities to practice the skills with Just in Time support.
3. Resource Phase—Building schema by gathering, organizing, and evaluating media examples as evidence for a proposition or as a theme based on an idea. Students should see exemplars at this point. These media examples are used during the collaboration phase as a shared reference for discussion.
   a. Think of the schema as a file folder in your brain with individual files for specific examples or processes, e.g., the dog schema could be the folder in your brain with specific sections for different types of dogs such as a basset hound and/or specific files for care of dogs.
   b. Students can gather online visual examples of the concept or term in order to build schema.
4. Collaboration Phase—Providing opportunities for students to discuss questions, debate ideas, and analyze propositions with each other and, if applicable, with practitioners using shared references as a basis for the discussion.
5. Production Phase—Providing opportunities to students to synthesize and build on knowledge by writing or authoring media products that answer the initial question, solve the problem, or communicate the decision.
6. Evaluative Phase—Students (and practitioners if applicable) evaluate and critique student work based on a rubric in order to further reinforce and maintain long-term memory acquisition of

knowledge, processes, and skills. Students are given opportunities to present their findings, solutions, or decisions through websites, oral presentations, podcasts, essays, books, etc. (Teachers keep exemplars for future learning opportunities.)

Money, Money, Money, Money

With all of these solutions, one might wonder how all these initiatives could be funded in these financially tight times in education. Thankfully, over the years government and district funding, such as Enhancing Education Through Technology and the Digital High School grant, has increased the number of computers in the classroom. Many schools have one computer for every five students as a result of these funding efforts. Other schools like those in the state of Maine have financed the purchase of one computer for every student (at certain grade levels). However, these funding sources are sporadic and don't address the total cost of owning a computer in education. These subsidies, often disbursed on a one-time only basis from the state or federal government, many times are not sufficient to deal with repair, software, and training costs. Frustrated teachers without adequate software for their students or without access because of broken computers are often forced to purchase their own equipment and software for their students or simply wait months before the overworked district technician arrives to repair the computer.

Consistent educational technology funding that addresses the total cost of owning educational technology is needed. The federal government, state government, and districts need to systematically address training, software, hardware, repair, infrastructure, and development costs for teachers to be able to successfully integrate technology into education.

However, many educators are not willing to wait until local and state governments are prepared to create policy addressing these financial issues. Of course there are numerous grants for which educators can apply. There are also many good resources addressing how teachers can apply for and receive grant monies. In addition to grants, one often underutilized resource forgotten by educators is the use of partnerships to leverage existing resources or even create new ones.

When we did our My So-Called Digital Life project, I remember early into the program presenting to a group of county, university, district, and school educators. After telling them about the project and the $250,000 price tag associated with it, I saw some people start squirming in their chairs. One very polite man from the county raised his hand and asked how we would get the $250,000 we needed for the project. I told him, "The companies and partners are going to give us the equipment, resources, training, and support. I'm expecting one of the major camera companies to give us 300 digital cameras." The disbelief was palpable in the room. However, we had a plan and I shared it with him and the others. These were the key components to the plan that I proposed at the meeting to get the money and other resources for the project.

1. Develop professionally produced materials (brochures, websites, video public service announcements) describing the project and defining what help we needed.
2. Define deliverables to sponsors and corporate sponsors such as advertising in newsletters, programs, banners, space on the website, etc.
3. Circulate press releases in papers, get public service announcements aired on CBS, send out hundreds of emails to vendors, businesses, parents, etc., inviting them to participate.
4. Form a consortium of partners that includes corporations, universities, parents, students, principals, teachers, professionals, and community leaders to support the project.
5. Do follow-up phone calls and set up information meetings with PTA, community organizations, corporate contacts, and university professors.
6. After meetings make follow-up phone calls.

After a couple months we had our committee in place, contacts made, website created, and our brochures professionally printed. Even though we had printed some pamphlets from our computer, partners didn't take us seriously until our brochures were professionally done. We started with people we knew or friends of friends who might be able to assist us. The donation from the printer for the brochures came to us because our secretary's husband worked in a print shop and he pitched the idea to the owner. We were able to develop the partnerships with Apple and Verizon after we contacted the sales representatives for our area and these representatives helped to set up meetings with division managers who were able to offer resources for the project. With each meeting the manager wanted to know what others had contributed. Each manager gave a little more than the previous partner. This progressive increase in resources came to a crescendo when Nikon gave 300 of their mid-range digital cameras to the students in our project. As we reflected back on our search for the needed partners to make this project possible, the very first contribution of $100 from our initial corporate sponsor was the reason that we ultimately got the last donation of the digital cameras. We saw that our small success made other larger successes possible. By leveraging the resources of corporations, professionals, parents, higher education, community leaders, and K-12 educators, we were able to acquire the needed technologies for the project. Whether the need is small or large, we must get our community involved.

AFTERWORD

EVEN THOUGH A RIGOROUS, community-connected, personal, and relevant education does provide a lens by which to potentially solve the problem of student disengagement and dropout, this approach misses the larger issue of why we as a nation are so committed to public education. By providing an education to the country's children, our sons and daughters will fulfill the hopes of a nation. Who do we want our children to become? How will our children create the new American Dream?

I was sitting on a wooden chair next to my grandfather's bed as he lay asleep, and I remembered the times when I would go into the butcher's shop as a young boy where he worked. Even though everyone else called me Bobby, he'd say, "Hello, Robert" (his middle name was Robert and I knew he saw a part of himself in me). Whenever he greeted me I could hear the pride in his voice as he told the other butchers and even the customers in the shop that I was his grandson. He always stopped his work for a moment to give me a piece of salami and share a joke or story. He laughed at his own humorous accounts, but what I liked more was how he laughed at my poorly delivered jokes. After a few minutes he'd have to go back to work and I would leave the shop with my father, a huge smile on my face, with the hope of seeing my grandfather soon. I never tired of visiting my grandfather and always looked forward to the next time I would see him.

Almost 20 years later, I had come from Southern California to visit my grandfather in Bullhead City, Arizona, for the last time. What was once a strong, large-framed man was now a frail 90-pound person in the last stages of terminal pancreatic cancer. I held his hand, and even though he was heavily medicated, he seemed to move between restless states of delirium and short moments of consciousness. One time he awoke and said, "Robert, I'm in so much pain." He moved quickly back into a state of delirium where he moaned and stirred constantly. His short moment of clarity cut me deeply, and I don't remember crying like that since I was boy. I went to my grandmother in the other room (he was on home hospice care) to tell her about his discomfort. She told me that the doctors didn't seem to be able to do anything for the pain.

How could it be that in this day with access to various pain-relieving technologies and medication that they couldn't figure out how to help him? From what my grandmother told me, I did not perceive the doctor as especially incompetent or uncaring but rather just painfully ordinary. They weren't the type of physicians that cared for multimillionaire CEO of Apple Inc. Steve Jobs, who sat comfortably sending email from his hospital room shortly after his bout with pancreatic cancer. My grandfather's physician didn't know how to cure the cancer or even how to medicate the pain. However, it didn't matter for much longer because my grandfather held on for only four more days before death finally eased the hurt. When my grandmother called me to let me know of his death, she told me about his last moments of clarity in which she said "he called you an angel who stayed and took care of him for those days." When I hung up, the boy in the butcher shop sat remembering the pride in his grandfather's voice at the man his grandson had become, and he smiled.

Who will our children become? Will they develop into the researchers and physicians that cure cancer, a CEO of an international company, an engineer that builds a high-rise that can't catch fire, or the President of the United States? What will our nation become? Will this be a country in which a doctor educated in our public schools can ease the pain of a dying grandparent? Will the daughter of a police officer or a nephew of a plumber hope to access and use the technologies of the elite? Could the son of a farm worker taught in a public school be given the knowledge to find a renewable energy source? Could a butcher's grandson become a teacher able to educate the daughter of a waitress and the son of a strawberry picker to become the next attorney general?

To diminish the importance and scope of education to merely the acquisition of perfunctory skills, our generation will forego our opportunity to create the America that every prior generation has dreamed for the next group of children. For over 200 years in America, each generation has passed the experiences, knowledge, arts, technologies, sciences, philosophies, values, and dreams from the collective community of present and past to the new, emerging generation in the hopes of reducing suffering, increasing prosperity, building united communities, and finding the answers to hidden mysteries. In this passing from one generation to the next, sons and daughters look into the reflection they cast in their parents' eyes to see the hopes that they can aspire to fulfill. When they look into our eyes, what hope do we cast for them?

INVENTORY FOR PARENTS

Survey I

Determine if your son or daughter is likely to be engaged in class.

This inventory is for a specific course or class rather than for school in general. Answer these questions with a particular course in mind.

1. Does your child think his or her teacher is interesting?
2. Does your child think he or she is good in the subject?
3. Does your child have an opportunity to discuss ideas with other classmates or with the teacher at least once a week during the class?
4. Does your child think this particular course is meaningful (either to their present life or to their future)?
5. Does your child feel connected to this particular teacher during class?

If you have answered no to two or more of these questions, your child is likely disengaged from learning in this particular class. (Disengaged means they are not paying attention, listening, or actively taking part in the class.)

Survey II

Determine if your son or daughter is at risk of dropping out.

Answer the questions in this inventory about your child's school experience in general (NOT for a particular course).

1. Does your child feel alone, isolated, or alienated from other students?
2. Does your child feel alienated from most of his or her teachers?
3. Does your child often feel confused in classes?
4. Does your child feel school is meaningless or irrelevant?

If you answered yes to two or more of these questions, your child is potentially at risk of dropping out.

INVENTORY FOR TEACHERS

Determine if your students are likely to be engaged in class.

This inventory is for a specific course or class rather than for school in general. Answer these questions with a particular course in mind.

1. Do you often present material in multisensory and visually rich formats?
2. Do you provide opportunities for students to present materials to and work with authentic audiences (e.g., presentation to students, parents, community)?
3. Do you allow for students to move through coursework at their own pace?
4. Do you allow hands-on learning opportunities on a weekly basis?
5. Do you often allow students to personalize their learning experience?
6. Do you often tell stories that are relevant to the concepts and material being taught?
7. Do you give your students weekly opportunities to discuss ideas in small groups or within the large group?
8. During independent practice, do you continuously answer questions or help individual or small groups of students?
9. Do your students feel that the learning is relevant to them?

If you have answered no to four or more of these questions, your students are likely to be disengaged from learning in this particular class. (Disengaged means they are not paying attention, listening, or actively taking part in the class.)

EDUCATIONAL RESOURCES

http://pixel.fhda.edu/id/six_facets.html
This website provides information, resources, and templates about how you would implement an Understanding By Design (UBD) lesson plan.

http://www.emazesolution.org/
This site provides an overview, media, samples, photographs, and lesson plans of the My So-Called Digital Life writing project.

http://www.aleks.com/
This site provides access to the ALEKS math program helping students in algebra and geometry. Individual students or classes of students can use this web-based program.

http://www.pearsondigital.com/successmaker/
This is a commercial product that has been effective at improving student achievement through their Computer Assisted Instruction math software for grades 2–7. The research indicates that typically 23 hours of using the program will increase student achievement by one grade level.

http://www.acmeanimation.org/
This nonprofit organization provides an opportunity for students to be mentored by professional animators from companies such as Warner Brothers through their website. Students submit their animations and artwork online and receive feedback about their creations.

http://www.globe.gov/globe_flash.html
Project Globe provides students with hands-on science education and access to other classrooms, educators, and scientists around the world.
http://www.earthkam.ucsd.edu/

EarthKAM is a NASA-sponsored website where students get the opportunity to direct a digital camera on select space flights as well as on the International Space Station.

http://www.qwizdom.com/index2.php
Qwizdom's commercial website provides information about the electronic response pads that enable teachers to get instant feedback about how their students are doing.

http://www.pltw.org/index.html
This Project Lead the Way website provides information about a middle and high school pre-engineering curriculum in which students get an opportunity to work with engineers on authentic projects.

http://www.youtube.com/
The YouTube website provides students with the opportunity to publish and download videos on the web.

http://www.epals.com/
EPALS is a free online web source for K-12 classrooms that establishes electronic penpals and email accounts so that students can communicate with other classes around the world.

https://www.blogger.com/start
Blogger is a free website that enables anyone to establish their own blogs and respond to other blogs.

http://en.wikibooks.org/wiki/Main_Page
This website provides further resources on current Wiki projects, such as online editable books.

http://www.secondlife.com/
The Second Life website provides online space for anyone to enter and create new virtual worlds.

http://www.nike.com/nikeplus/
The Nike Plus website allows for real-time data from your running workout to be collected and uploaded to track progress.

SELECTED REFERENCES

Adams, J. T. 2001. *The epic of America.* Simon Publications.

American Institute of Physics. 2005. President Bush proposes new education initiative. *The AIP Bulletin of Science Policy News.* http://www.aip.org/fyi/2005/012.html

American Youth Policy. 2001. Proceedings from American Society for Engineering Education Annual Conference and Exposition. http://www.asee.org/acPapers/00094_2001.PDF

Anderson, G. 1994. *Studying your own school: An educator's guide to qualitative practitioner research.* Thousand Oaks, CA: Corwin Press.

Artz, A. F., and C. M. Newman. 1990. Cooperative learning. *Mathematics Teacher* 83: 448–449.

Bandura, A. 1977. *Social learning theory.* Upper Saddle River, NJ: Prentice.

Barksdale-Ladd, M., and K. Thomas. 2000. What's at stake in high stakes testing: Teachers and parents speak out. *Journal of Teacher Education* 51: 384–398.

Barton, P. Policy Information Center of Educational Testing Service. 2005. *One-third of a nation: Rising dropout rates and declining opportunities.* Princeton, NJ: Policy Information Center of Educational Testing Service. http://www.ets.org/Media/Education_Topics/pdf/onethird.pdf (accessed October 10, 2005).

Battistich, V., M. Watson, D. Solomon, E. Schaps, and J. Solomon. 1991. The child development project: A comprehensive program for the development of prosocial character. In *Handbook of moral behavior and development: Application, Vol 3*, ed. W. M. Kurtines and J. L. Gewirtz, 1–34. Hillsdale, NJ: Lawrence Erlbaum.

Bereiter, C., C. Brett, P. J. Burtis, C. Calhoun, M. Scardamalia, and N. Smith Lea. 1992. Educational applications of a networked communal database. *Interactive Learning Environments* 2 (1): 45–71.

Bereiter, C., and M. Scardamalia. 1987. *The psychology of written composition*. Hillsdale, NJ: Lawrence Erlbaum Associates.

Berman, S. 1997. *Children's social consciousness and the development of social responsibility*. Albany, NY: State University of New York Press.

Bernard, R. H. 2001. *Research methods in anthropology: Qualitative and quantitative approaches*. Walnut Creek, CA: Altamira Press.

Bogdan, R.C., and S. K. Bilken. 1992. *Qualitative research for education*. 2nd ed. Boston: Allyn & Bacon.

Bransford, J., A. Brown, and R. Cocking. 1999. *How people learn*. National Research Council. Washington, DC: National Academy Press.

Center for Evaluation and Education Policy. 2005. High school survey of student engagement. http://www.indiana.edu/~ceep/hssse/pdf/hssse_2005_report.pdf

Clark, R. 1999. The CANE model of work motivation: A two-stage model of commitment and necessary mental effort. In *Trends in corporate training*, ed. J. Lowyck. Leuven, Belgium: University of Leuven Press.

Cohen, M., and M. Riel. 1989. The effect of distant audiences on students' writing. *American Educational Research Journal* 26 (2): 143–159.

Coles, G. 2001. Learning to read—"Scientifically." *Rethinking Schools Online* 15 (4). http://www.rethinkingschools.org/archive/15_04/Read154.shtml.

Collier, J., and C. Malcolm. 1986. *Visual anthropology: Photography as a research method.* Albuquerque, NM: University of New Mexico Press.

Cothran, D., and C. Ennis. 2000. Building bridges to student engagement: Communicating respect and care for students in urban high schools. *Journal of Research and Development in Education* 33 (2).

Cradler, J., M. McNabb, M. Freeman, and R. Burchett. 2002. How does technology influence student learning? *Learning & Leading with Technology* 29 (8): 46–49, 56.

Crook, C. 1994. *Computers and the collaborative experience of learning.* New York: Routledge.

Cuban, L. 2001. *Oversold and underused: Computers in the classroom.* Cambridge, MA: Harvard University Press.

Daphne, J. W., and L. Hsiao. 2003. CSCL theories. University of Texas website. http://www.edb.utexas.edu/csclstudent/Dhsiao/theories.html#csile (accessed August 10, 2003).

Dewey, J. 1990. *The school and society and the child and the curriculum.* Chicago, IL: University of Chicago Press.

Driscoll, M. P. 2002. How people learn (and what technology might have to do with it). *ERIC Digest.* Syracuse, NY: ERIC Clearinghouse on Information and Technology.

Eden, H. 2003. Getting in on the (inter)action: Exploring affordances for collaborative learning in a context of informed participation. University of Colorado at Boulder website. http://newmedia.colorado.edu/cscl/186.html (accessed August 8, 2003).

Ellis, A. 2001. Student-centered collaborative learning via face-to-face and asynchronous online communication: What's the difference? Proceedings from FLITE Center Conference, Victoria, Australia.

Ewald, W. 1992. *Magic eyes: Scenes from an Andean girlhood.* Seattle: Bay Press.

———. 1996. *I dreamed I had a girl in my pocket: The story of an Indian village,* with stories and photographs by the children of Vichya, India. New York: Doubletake Books and W.W. Norton.

Gamoran, A., and M. Nystrand. 1992. Taking students seriously. In *Student engagement and achievement in American secondary schools,* ed. F. M. Newmann, 40–61. New York: Teachers College Press.

Gates, B. 2005. Prepared remarks for National Education Summit on High Schools. http://www.gatesfoundation.org/MediaCenter/Speeches/Co-Chair Speeches/BillgSpeeches/BGSpeechNGA-050226.htm

Gee, J. P. 2003. *What video games have to teach us about learning and literacy.* New York: Palgrave Macmillan.

Glickman, C. 2006. Proceedings from the ACSA Conference, Anaheim, CA.

Goetz, J. P., and M. D. LeCompte. 1981. Ethnographic research and the problem of data reduction. *Anthropology and Education Quarterly* 12 (1): 51–70.

———. 1984. *Ethnography and qualitative design in educational research.* Orlando, FL: Academic Press.

Hausfather, S. J. 1996. Vygotsky and schooling: Creating a social context for learning. *Action in Teacher Education* 18 (2): 1–10.

Hirsch, E. D., Jr. 1988. *Cultural literacy: What every American needs to know.* New York: Vintage Books.

Johnson, D. W., and R. T. Johnson. 1999. What makes cooperative learning work. In *JALT applied materials: Cooperative learning,* ed. D. Kluge, S. McGuire, D. Johnson and R. Johnson, 23–36. Japan: Japan Association for Language Learning.

Johnson, D. W., R. T. Johnson, E. Holubec, and P. Roy. 1984. *Circles of learning: Cooperation in the classroom.* Alexandria, VA: Association for Supervision and Curriculum Development.

Jones, G., B. Jones, and T. Hargrove. 2003. *The unintended consequences of high-stakes testing.* Lanham, MD: Rowman & Littlefield.

Kansas City Star. 2006. Young engineers build their futures: Project Lead the Way will expand to more schools, giving students hands-on experience. June 6.

Kim, J. 2005. Reading Research proceedings from UCI: Research Symposium.

Klem, A. M., and J. C. Connell. 2003. *Relationships matter: Linking teacher support to student engagement and achievement.* Philadelphia: Institute for Research and Reform in Education.

Kolodner, J., and M. Guzdial. 1996. Effects with and of CSCL: Tracking learning in a new paradigm. In *CSCL: Theory and practice of an emerging paradigm,* ed. T. Koschmann, 307–320. Mahwah, NJ: Lawrence Erlbaum Associates.

Koschmann, T. 1996. Paradigm shifts and instructional technology: An introduction. In *CSCL: Theory and practice of an emerging paradigm,* ed. T. Koschmann, 1–24. Mahwah, NJ: Lawrence Erlbaum Associates.

———. 2001. *Revisiting the paradigms of instructional technology.* Mahwah, NJ: Lawrence Erlbaum Associates.

Kuhn, A. 1995. *Family secrets: Acts of memory and imagination.* New York: Verso.

Kulik, J. A. 2002. *School mathematics and science programs benefit from instructional technology.* National Science Foundation InfoBrief report, NSF 03-301. http://dwbrr.unl.edu/iTech/TEAC859/Read/KulikTech.pdf (accessed September 21, 2005).

La Rose, R., J. Greff, and M. Eastin. 1998. Audiographic telecourses for the web: An experiment. *Journal of Computer-Mediated Communication* 4 (2): 122–132.

Lave, J., and E. Wenger. 1991. *Situated learning: Legitimate peripheral participation.* New York: Cambridge University Press.

Li, Q. 2002. Exploration of collaborative learning and communication in an educational environment using computer-mediated communication. *Journal of Research on Technology in Education* 34 (4): 503–516.

Liethwood, K., D. Jantzi, and P. Haskell. 1997. Developing the organizational learning capacity of school systems: A case study (Notes for presentation). Paper presented at the annual meeting of the University Council for Educational Administration, Orlando, FL.

Lincoln, Y., and E. Guba. 1985. *Naturalistic inquiry.* New York: Sage.

Lykes, M. 2001. Creative arts and photography in participatory action research in Guatemala. In *Handbook of action research: Participative inquiry and practice,* ed. P. Reason and H. Bradbury, 363–371. London: Sage.

Marks, H. 2000. Student engagement in instructional activity: Patterns in the elementary, middle, and high school years. *American Educational Research Journal* 37 (1): 153–184.

Means, B., C. Korbak, A. Lewis, V. Michalchik, W. R. Penuel, J. Rollin, and L. Yarnall. 2000. *GLOBE year 5 evaluation: Classroom practices.* Menlo Park, CA: SRI International. http://www.globe.gov/fsl/evals/y5full.pdf (accessed October 17, 2004)

Merriam, S. 1988. *Case study research in education: A qualitative approach.* San Francisco, CA: Jossey-Bass.

Metz, J. M. 1992. *Computer-mediated communication: Perceptions of a new context.* Paper presented at the Speech Communication Association annual conference, Chicago, IL.

National Aeronautics and Space Administration. 2004. Exploring Earth with EarthKam. http://www.nasa.gov/audience/forstudents/5-8/features/ F_EarthKAM_5-8.html (accessed October 10, 2004).

National Center for Education Statistics. 2002. Public libraries in the United States: Fiscal year 2002. *Education Statistics Quarterly* 7 (1–2). http://nces.ed.gov/programs/quarterly/vol_7/1_2/7_3.asp (accessed August 8, 2005).

National Governors Association/Achieve High School Summit. 2006. Bill and Melinda Gates Foundation. Education program fact sheet. http://www.gatesfoundation.org/Education/RelatedInfo/EducationFact Sheet-021201.htm

National Governors Association. 2005. Graduation counts: A report of the NGA Task Force on state high school graduation data. Washington, DC: National Governors Association. http://www.nga.org/portal/site/nga/ menuitem.9123e83a1f6786440ddcbeeb501010a0/?vgnextoid=7cadf891b c025010VgnVCM1000001a01010aRCRD

National Institute of Child Health and Human Development. 2000. Report of the National Reading Panel: Teaching children to read. Washington, DC: U.S. Government Printing Office.

National Research Council and the Institute of Medicine. 2004. *Engaging schools: Fostering high school students' motivation to learn.* Washington, DC: The National Academies Press.

North Central Regional Education Laboratory. 2003. enGauge® 21st century skills: Literacy in the digital age. http://www.ncrel.org/ engauge/skills/techlit.htm.

Nuthall, G. 1997. Learning how to learn: The social construction of knowledge acquisition in the classroom. Paper presented at the Biennial Conference of the European Association for Research in Learning and Instruction.

O'Brien, E. 2004. Effects of computer-mediated communication on student achievement. Master's thesis, National University, La Jolla, CA.

Oppenheimer, T. 2003. *The flickering mind: The false promise of technology in the classroom and how learning can be saved.* New York: Random House.

Osterman, K. 2000. Students' need for belongingness in the school community. *Review of Educational Research* 70 (3): 323–36.

Patrick, S. 2005. Educators driving change in communities: Creating new uses for technology and impacting economic development. Symposium conducted at Education Visionary, Washington, DC.

Patton, M. Q. 1990. *Qualitative evaluation and research methods.* 2nd ed. Newbury Park, CA: Sage.

Perkins, D. N., and G. Salomon. 1988. Teaching for transfer. *Educational Leadership* 46 (1): 22–32.

Prensky, M. 2001. Digital natives, digital immigrants part 1. *On the Horizon* 9 (5).

Press Enterprise. 2006. Beating video shows the power of YouTube. November.

Reuters. 2006. Microsoft's Zune off to a slow start. FoxNews.com, November 15. http://www.foxnews.com/printer_friendly_story/0,3566,229580,00.html

Salovaara, H., P. Salo, M. Rahikainen, L. Lipponen, and S. Jarvela. 2001. Developing technology-supported inquiry practices in two comprehensive school classrooms. Proceedings from the world conference on Educational Multimedia, Hypermedia & Telecommunications, Tampere, Finland.

Scardamalia, M. 2000. Can schools enter a knowledge society? In *Educational technology and the impact on teaching and learning,* ed. M. Selinger and J. Wynn, 5–9. Abingdon, Oxon, England: Research Machines PLC.

Scardamalia, M., and C. Bereiter. 1996. Computer support for knowledge building communities. In *CSCL: Theory and practice of an emerging paradigm*, ed. T. Koschmann, 249–268. Mahwah, NJ: Lawrence Erlbaum Associates.

Scardamalia, M., C. Bereiter, and M. Lamon. 2001. Mapping learning and the growth. American Educational Research Association Meeting. http://ikit.org/lamon/mapping.html (accessed October 9, 2004).

Schmoker, M. 2001. *The results fieldbook: Practical strategies from dramatically improved schools.* Alexandria, VA: Association for Supervision and Curriculum Development.

Skinner, B. F. 1978. *Reflections on behavioralism and society.* Englewood Cliffs, NJ: Prentice-Hall.

Slavin, R. 1990. *Cooperative learning: Theory, research and practice.* Englewood Cliffs, NJ: Prentice-Hall.

———. 1995. *Cooperative learning: Theory, research, and practice.* 2nd ed. Boston: Allyn & Bacon.

Spence, J., and J. Solomon, eds. 1995. *What can a woman do with a camera?* London: Scarlet Press.

Strauss, A. L., and J. Corbin. 1990. *Basics of qualitative research: Grounded theory procedures and techniques.* Newbury Park, CA: Sage.

Strauss, N., and W. Howe. 2000. *Millennials Rising.* New York: Vintage.

Stringer, E. T. 1999. *Action Research: A handbook for practitioners.* 2nd ed. Newbury Park, CA: Sage.

Tao, P. K. 2000. Computer supported collaborative physics learning: Developing understanding of image formation by lenses. Proceedings from Research Colloquium 2000, Hong Kong.

Tao, P. K., and R. F. Gunstone. 1999. Conceptual change in science through collaborative learning at the computer. *International Journal of Science Education* 21 (1): 39–57.

Tudge, J., and D. Hogan. 1997. Collaboration from a Vygotskian perspective. Proceedings from symposium at the biennial meetings of the Society for Research in Child Development, North Carolina.

United States Department of Education. 2005. Dropout Prevention Program Recognition Initiative. http://www.ed.gov/programs/dropout/dropoutprogram.html (accessed November 1, 2005).

United States Department of Education. Office of the Secretary. 2001. *No child left behind.* Washington, DC: Government Printing Office.

Van Aalst, J., C. Chan, and E. Lee. 2001. Assessing and fostering knowledge building inquiry and discourse. Simon Fraser University website. http://www.educ.sfu.ca/kb/Papers/Chan_vanAalst01.pdf (accessed May 1, 2004).

Vars, G. F., and J. A. Beane. 2000. Integrative curriculum in a standards-based world. *ERIC Digest.* Champaign, IL: ERIC Clearinghouse on Elementary and Early Childhood Education.

Verillon, P. 2000. Revisiting Piaget and Vygotsky: In search of a learning model for technology education. *Journal of Technology Studies* 26 (1): 3–10.

Vygotsky, L. S. 1978. *Mind in society: The development of higher psychological processes.* Cambridge: Harvard University Press.

Wang, M., J. Laffey, P. Wangemann, C. Harris, and T. Tupper. 2000. How do youth and mentors experience project-based learning in the Internet-based shared environment for expeditions (iExpeditions)? Paper presented at the annual meeting of the American Education Research Association, New Orleans, LA.

Warschauer, M. 2003. *Technology and social inclusion: Rethinking the digital divide.* Cambridge, MA: The MIT Press.

Wasson, B. 1998. *Computer supported collaborative learning: An overview.* http://www.ifi.uib.no/staff/barbara/publications-list.htm (accessed August 9, 2003).

Weber, S. J., and C. A. Mitchell. 2004. Using visual and artistic modes of representation for self-study. In *International handbook of self-study of teaching and teacher education practices*, ed. J. Loughran, M. Hamilton, V. LaBoskey, and T. Russell, 979–1037. Dordrecht, Netherlands: Kluwer Press.

Wiggins, G., and J. McTighe. 2001. *Understanding by design.* New York: Prentice Hall Inc.

Wilgus, B. C. P. 2002. The relationship of peer collaboration on third grade student math performance. Master's thesis, Johnson Bible College. *ERIC Digest.* http://www.eric.ed.gov/ERICDocs/data/ericdocs2/content_storage_01/0000000b/80/27/ed/8a.pdf.

Ziller, R.C. 1990. *Photographing the self: Methods for observing personal orientations.* Newbury Park, CA: Sage.

PHOTO CREDITS

Front cover (left to right): Photos by Kathy DeLeon, Danica Lopez, Raqul Lucero, and Stefy Nudel

Page 12: Photo by Joseph Won

Page 13: Photo by Ryan Mac

Page 15: Photo by Roxanne Talamayan

Page 18: Photo by Y-Lan "Laney" Tran

Page 20: Photo by Michael J.

Page 27: Photo by Araceli Valencia

Page 28: Photo by Francis Inocelda

Page 39: Photo by Dillon Chaffin

Page 53: Photo by Sean Mooney

Page 65: Photo by Amber M.

Page 67: Photo by Min Young Park

Page 69: Photo by Daniel Koval

Page 76: Photo by Amber M

Page 81: Photo by Danica Lopez

Page 83: Photo by Carolina Rosales

Page 85: Photo by Katy DeLeon

Page 86: Photo by Araceli Valencia

Page 117: Photo by David Pletka

MY SO-CALLED DIGITAL LIFE

2,000 TEENAGERS, 300 CAMERAS, AND 30 DAYS TO DOCUMENT THEIR WORLD

CREATED BY BOB PLETKA

My So-Called Digital Life is the result of a unique program in which 2,000 high school and middle school students from throughout the state of California—including urban, suburban, and rural areas—were given digital cameras and one month to capture their day-to-day life experiences. The teenagers also contributed essays, photo captions, and artwork to the project.

"Adults and teens will come away stirred and enlightened by this raw, impressive student collaboration and by Pletka's moving introduction, which challenges administrators to rethink how school is taught."—*Booklist*

"An honest, colorful and poignant book. It captures high school life the way it really is, not the shiny way you see it on Fox."—*San Diego Union-Tribune*

"This book serves as a broad, almost panoramic collage of the edgy, high-tech lives of teenagers in the early 21st century."—*Library Journal*

$24.95 • Trade Paper • ISBN 1-595800-05-0 • 176 pages • 11 x 8 1/2 • Hundreds of Color Photographs • Photography/Education

CALL 1-800-784-9553 TO ORDER

BOOKS AVAILABLE FROM SANTA MONICA PRESS

The Bad Driver's Handbook
Hundreds of Simple Maneuvers to Frustrate, Annoy, and Endanger Those Around You
by Zack Arnstein and Larry Arnstein
192 pages $12.95

Calculated Risk
The Extraordinary Life of Jimmy Doolittle
by Jonna Doolittle Hoppes
360 pages $24.95

Captured!
Inside the World of Celebrity Trials
by Mona Shafer Edwards
176 pages $24.95

Creepy Crawls
A Horror Fiend's Travel Guide
by Leon Marcelo
384 pages $16.95

Educating the Net Generation
How to Engage Students in the 21st Century
by Bob Pletka
168 pages $16.95

The Encyclopedia of Sixties Cool
A Celebration of the Grooviest People, Events, and Artifacts of the 1960s
by Chris Strodder
336 pages $24.95

Exotic Travel Destinations for Families
by Jennifer M. Nichols and Bill Nichols
360 pages $16.95

Footsteps in the Fog
Alfred Hitchcock's San Francisco
by Jeff Kraft and Aaron Leventhal
240 pages $24.95

French for Le Snob
Adding Panache to Your Everyday Conversations
by Yvette Reche
400 pages $16.95

Haunted Hikes
Spine-Tingling Tales and Trails from North America's National Parks
by Andrea Lankford
376 pages $16.95

How to Speak Shakespeare
by Cal Pritner and Louis Colaianni
144 pages $16.95

Jackson Pollock
Memories Arrested in Space
by Martin Gray
216 pages $14.95

James Dean Died Here
The Locations of America's Pop Culture Landmarks
by Chris Epting
312 pages $16.95

L.A. Noir
The City as Character
by Alain Silver and James Ursini
176 pages $19.95

Led Zeppelin Crashed Here
The Rock and Roll Landmarks of North America
by Chris Epting
336 pages $16.95

Loving Through Bars
Children with Parents in Prison
by Cynthia Martone
216 pages $21.95

Movie Star Homes
by Judy Artunian and Mike Oldham
312 pages $16.95

My So-Called Digital Life
2,000 Teenagers, 300 Cameras, and 30 Days to Document Their World
by Bob Pletka
176 pages $24.95

Offbeat Museums
The Collections and Curators of America's Most Unusual Museums
by Saul Rubin
240 pages $19.95

A Prayer for Burma
by Kenneth Wong
216 pages $14.95

Quack!
Tales of Medical Fraud from the Museum of Questionable Medical Devices
by Bob McCoy
240 pages $19.95

Redneck Haiku
Double-Wide Edition
by Mary K. Witte
240 pages $11.95

Route 66 Adventure Handbook
by Drew Knowles
312 pages $16.95

The Ruby Slippers, Madonna's Bra, and Einstein's Brain
The Locations of America's Pop Culture Artifacts
by Chris Epting
312 pages $16.95

School Sense
How to Help Your Child Succeed in Elementary School
by Tiffani Chin, Ph.D.
408 pages $16.95

The Shakespeare Diaries
A Fictional Autobiography
by J.P. Wearing
456 pages $27.95

Silent Echoes
Discovering Early Hollywood Through the Films of Buster Keaton
by John Bengtson
240 pages $24.95

Silent Traces
Discovering Early Hollywood Through the Films of Charlie Chaplin
by John Bengtson
304 pages $24.95

Tiki Road Trip, 2nd Edition
by James Teitelbaum
360 pages $16.95

ORDER FORM 1-800-784-9553

	Quantity	Amount
The Bad Driver's Handbook ($12.95)	_____	_____
Calculated Risk ($24.95)	_____	_____
Captured! ($24.95)	_____	_____
Creepy Crawls ($16.95)	_____	_____
Educating the Net Generation ($16.95)	_____	_____
The Encyclopedia of Sixties Cool ($24.95)	_____	_____
Exotic Travel Destinations for Families ($16.95)	_____	_____
Footsteps in the Fog: Alfred Hitchcock's San Francisco ($24.95)	_____	_____
French for Le Snob ($16.95)	_____	_____
Haunted Hikes ($16.95)	_____	_____
How to Speak Shakespeare ($16.95)	_____	_____
Jackson Pollock: Memories Arrested in Space ($14.95)	_____	_____
James Dean Died Here: America's Pop Culture Landmarks ($16.95)	_____	_____
L.A. Noir: The City as Character ($19.95)	_____	_____
Led Zeppelin Crashed Here ($16.95)	_____	_____
Loving Through Bars ($21.95)	_____	_____
Movie Star Homes ($16.95)	_____	_____
My So-Called Digital Life ($24.95)	_____	_____
Offbeat Museums ($19.95)	_____	_____
A Prayer for Burma ($14.95)	_____	_____
Quack! Tales of Medical Fraud ($19.95)	_____	_____
Redneck Haiku ($11.95)	_____	_____
Route 66 Adventure Handbook ($16.95)	_____	_____
The Ruby Slippers, Madonna's Bra, and Einstein's Brain ($16.95)	_____	_____
School Sense ($16.95)	_____	_____
The Shakespeare Diaries ($27.95)	_____	_____
Silent Echoes: Early Hollywood Through Buster Keaton ($24.95)	_____	_____
Silent Traces (24.95)	_____	_____
Tiki Road Trip, 2nd Edition ($16.95)	_____	_____

	Subtotal	_____
Shipping & Handling:	CA residents add 8.25% sales tax	_____
1 book $4.00	Shipping and Handling (see left)	_____
Each additional book is $1.00	TOTAL	_____

Name _____

Address _____

City _____ State _____ Zip _____

❒ Visa ❒ MasterCard   Card No.: _____

Exp. Date _____ Signature _____

❒ Enclosed is my check or money order payable to:

Santa Monica Press LLC
P.O. Box 1076
Santa Monica, CA 90406

www.santamonicapress.com 1-800-784-9553